THE EXERCISE
OF THE
KINGDOM
FOR THE
BUILDING
OF THE
CHURCH

WITNESS LEE

Living Stream Ministry
Anaheim, CA • www.lsm.org

First Edition, November 1989.

ISBN 978-0-87083-476-9

Published by

Living Stream Ministry
2431 W. La Palma Ave., Anaheim, CA 92801 U.S.A.
P. O. Box 2121, Anaheim, CA 92814 U.S.A.

Printed in the United States of America

15   16   17   18   19   /   10   9   8   7   6   5   4

CONTENTS

Title	*Page*
Preface	5
1 The Christ and the Son of the Living God	7
2 The Constitution of the Church and the Kingdom	15
3 Denying the Self for the Building of the Church	23
4 Bearing the Cross for the Building of the Church	33
5 Losing the Soul for the Building of the Church	43
6 The Salvation of the Soul	53
7 The Kingdom as an Exercise and a Reward	65
8 The Incentive to Seek Christ	79

PREFACE

This book is composed of messages given by Brother Witness Lee in Anaheim, California, in March and April 1978.

CHAPTER ONE

THE CHRIST AND THE SON
OF THE LIVING GOD

In this book we shall be concerned with Matthew 16, one of the greatest chapters in the Bible. In this chapter Christ is revealed in an extraordinary way, and the church is mentioned for the first time. This chapter also speaks of such things as the gates of Hades, the keys of the kingdom, and the building of the church upon the rock with so many Peters as the stones. In Matthew 16:13-28 there are at least eighteen crucial items: Christ, the church, the kingdom, the gates of Hades, the keys of the kingdom, the rock, the stone, the building of the church, the crucifixion, the resurrection, Satan, self-denial, the bearing of the cross, the losing or saving of the soul, the following of the Lord, the reward in the kingdom, the coming of the Son of Man, and the coming of the Son of Man in His kingdom. In this chapter we shall deal with the revelation of Christ in Matthew 16.

THE REVELATION OF CHRIST

Prior to Matthew 16 the Lord had been with His disciples for a period of time. During this time, He walked with them, conversed with them, dwelt with them, and ate with them. As a result, they came to know Him very well. Nevertheless, one day He took these disciples, who knew Him thoroughly, far away from the holy city and the holy temple to Caesarea Philippi, a region where the sky is clear and the atmosphere fresh. In this atmosphere He asked them a question: "Who do men say that the Son of Man is?" (v. 13). They replied, "Some, John the Baptist; and others, Elijah; and still others, Jeremiah or one of the prophets" (v. 14). All these nonsensical answers were spoken according to the natural, religious mentality. Instead of rebuking His disciples for these answers, He directed the question to them: "But you, who do you say that I am?" (v. 15). Then, to the surprise of the other disciples, Peter answered, "You are the Christ, the Son of the living God" (v. 16).

The definite article before the word *Christ* is very important. *Christ* is the anglicized form of the Greek word *Christos,* which is equivalent to the Hebrew word *Messiah.* Both *Messiah* in Hebrew and *Christos* in Greek mean "the anointed One." The term *Messiah,* the anointed One, is used in Daniel 9:26, which says, "After the sixty-two weeks Messiah will be cut off and will have nothing." All Bible students agree that this refers to Jesus Christ, who is the anointed One.

According to the Old Testament principle, anyone used by God to carry out His administration had to be anointed. Thus, the kings, priests, and prophets were all anointed when they came into function. This indicates that the anointing is for the carrying out of God's administration. Whatever God wants us to do or accomplish is related to His anointing. The ointment with which we are anointed actually is God Himself. God anoints us with Himself. God, however, is not simple, but complex. He is triune, that is, one in three and three in one. Although it is a fact that God is triune, this is a fact that no one can explain.

WATER FOR LIFE
AND OIL FOR FUNCTION

Peter declared not only that Jesus is the Christ but also that He is the Son of the living God. Christ is the anointed One, the One upon whom God has poured Himself out as the ointment to accomplish His administration. In the Bible, water, in its positive significance, indicates life, and oil indicates function. Both water and oil are used to represent the Spirit. The difference between these two symbols of the Spirit is that the Spirit as water is for life, whereas the Spirit as oil is for function. When the Spirit as water enters into you, that is for life. But when the Spirit as oil is poured upon you, that is for function. The Spirit as water getting into us is related to the Son of the living God, who is for life. The Spirit as oil poured upon us is related to the Christ. For the fulfillment of God's administration, we have life inwardly and function outwardly. Inwardly we have the Spirit who is water to be life to us, and outwardly we have the Spirit as oil upon us for function, for administration, and for the accomplishment of God's purpose. Our body has both life and function. Within our body there is life, and outwardly there are many functions. Likewise, on the one hand, God is life, and, on the other hand, He is function.

In Matthew 16 we have Christ with God poured upon Him as the ointment. On the day Christ was baptized, John the Baptist saw the Spirit of God descend upon Him (3:16). The Spirit came not as water but as oil, because Christ was the anointed One of God for the accomplishment of God's eternal purpose.

God is both living and working. For God to be living, there is life; but for God to be working, there is ointment. Jesus is the Christ for God's moving and administration; He is also the Son of the living God for life. First John 5:12 says, "He who has the Son has the life." We all need to look to the Lord for the heavenly revelation of these things.

John 14:23 Jesus answered and said to him, if anyone loves Me, he will keep My word, and My Father will love him, and We will come to him and make our abode with him.

REVEALED BY THE FATHER IN THE HEAVENS

Thank you Lord. I love You.

The Lord said to Peter, "Blessed are you, Simon Barjona, because flesh and blood has not revealed this to you, but My Father who is in the heavens" (Matt. 16:17). The Lord seemed to be saying, "You are Simon, the son of Jonah, the son of a man of flesh and blood. But flesh and blood did not reveal this matter to you. It was the Father in the heavens who revealed it." We need to look to the Father in the heavens to grant us to see that Jesus is the Christ and the Son of the living God. We need the Father to show us that Christ has the water, the life, and also the oil, the function. Do not assume that you know that Jesus is the Christ and the Son of the living God. This may be merely terminology to you. You may not yet have the revelation. When we were in Sunday school, we were taught that Jesus was the Christ and the Son of God. However, these terms did not mean anything to us. We need the revelation that the very Jesus in whom we believe for salvation is the Christ, the oil upon us for functioning, and the Son of the living God, the water within us for life.

John 14:21 He who has My commandments and keeps them, he is the one who loves Me; and he who loves Me will be loved by My Father, and I will love him and will manifest Myself to him.

RECEIVING THE SON AS LIFE

First John 5:12 says that he who has the Son has the life. The Son is the very life because He is the embodiment of God. Because God's element, essence, life, and nature are embodied in the Son, the Son is the substance, the expression, of the divine life. Therefore, if we have the Son, we have the divine life, the divine essence. If we have the Son, we have God in us as our life.

FIRMLY ATTACHED TO THE ANOINTED ONE

Second Corinthians 1:21 says, "The One who firmly attaches us with you unto Christ and has anointed us is God." By being attached to Christ, the anointed One, we have the ointment for function. Do not say that you are not able to pray in the meetings or give a testimony. If you have this concept, heaven will be closed to you. Oh, we all must look to the Lord for an open heaven! Forget about what you are or what you can do, and remember that you have received the Son of the living God into you as your life and that you have been attached to the anointed One. Because you have been attached to Him, the ointment upon Him is flowing down to you. Forget your weakness, dullness, or sense of nothingness. Although we are nothing, we have been attached to the anointed One. We have the Son of the living God within us, and we have been attached to the Christ. Thus, we have life within and ointment without. Anyone who believes this is truly blessed by the Father in the heavens.

TWO SOURCES

By nature we all are Barjonas, natural men born of natural fathers. But we also have another source, the Father in heaven. We, the followers of Christ, have two sources: a natural source and a heavenly source. On the one hand, we are Barjonas; on the other hand, we are sons of God. The Father in the heavens always cooperates with His Son. When the Son brought the disciples to Caesarea Philippi, the Father was ready to inspire Simon Barjona to see that Jesus, the Nazarene, is the Christ and the Son of the living God. Through this revelation Peter was transformed from Simon to Peter, from a son of Jonah to a son of the Father in the heavens. Thus, Peter received blessing from another source, from the Father in the heavens.

THIS ROCK

Matthew 16:18 may be translated as follows: "I also say to you that you are a stone, and on this rock I will build My church, and the gates of Hades shall not prevail against it." The Lord told Simon that he was a stone and that He would build the church upon this rock. This rock first refers to the wonderful person of Christ, the Son of the living God, the One who is our life and who has the oil. Second, it refers to the revelation of this person seen by Peter. When we see this revelation, the revelation becomes the rock. Thus, the church is built not only on the person but also on the revelation of this person. Third, this rock refers to Peter's declaration that Jesus is the Christ, the Son of the living God. Hence, the rock refers to three things: the person, the revelation, and the declaration.

THE WAY TO BE BUILT

Many Christians in Catholicism or in the denominations are familiar with the verse about Christ building His church upon this rock. However, they do not know how to be built upon this rock. In order to be built we need the person, the revelation, and the declaration. We should not only know this as a doctrine but also practice it. The person is always available, for He is both universal and local. But it is possible to talk about Christ without having the revelation of Him. As soon as we see that Jesus is the Christ, the Son of the living God, and declare it, we are built. However, nominal Christians who attend a so-called service on Sunday morning only to spend the rest of the day at sporting events or the movies are not built upon this rock. But when some begin to see that Jesus is the Christ and the Son of the living God, they are built up; for they are attached to Christ, the anointed One, and the Son of God comes into them as life. Immediately, they and He become one. It was at the juncture of confessing that Jesus was the Christ and the Son of God that Simon was changed to Peter.

DRINKING THE WATER
FLOWING FROM THE CLEFT ROCK

Although you may not realize it, 1 and 2 Corinthians are the continuation of Matthew 16. First Corinthians speaks of Christ and the rock, and 2 Corinthians mentions the anointed One. In 1 Corinthians 1:13 Paul asks, "Is Christ divided?" and in 12:12 he says, "Even as the body is one and has many members, yet all the members of the body, being many, are one body, so also is the Christ." First Corinthians 10:4 speaks of the rock: "All drank the same spiritual drink; for they drank of a spiritual rock which followed them, and the rock was Christ." This cleft rock out of which water flows is the very foundation mentioned in 1 Corinthians 3:11, where Paul says, "Another foundation no one is able to lay besides that which is laid, which is Jesus Christ." If we put these points together, we shall see how to be built upon this rock. According to Matthew 16, to be built upon this rock is to see the person, to receive the revelation, and to make the declaration. This, however, is the initial stage. We need to see further that this rock is the cleft rock out of which living water is flowing.

The rock being cleft signifies Christ crucified, and the flowing of living water signifies Christ flowing through resurrection. The river flowing out of the rock is designated in 1 Corinthians 15:45 as the life-giving Spirit. Hence, the life-giving Spirit is the water flowing out of the cleft rock. The crucified Christ is now flowing out the life-giving Spirit in His resurrection. First Corinthians 12:13 says, "In one Spirit we were all baptized into one Body, whether Jews or Greeks, whether slaves or free, and were all given to drink one Spirit." We all have been positioned to drink of this flowing water. Therefore, we continue to be built upon this rock by drinking the water flowing out of the cleft rock.

BEING BUILT BY DRINKING
AND REMAINING ATTACHED

As we have seen, 2 Corinthians 1:21 says that we have been attached to the anointed One. Thus, the continuation of the building unveiled in Matthew 16 is in the drinking and the attaching. Day by day we are drinking the water flowing out of the cleft rock, and we are also being attached to the anointed One. We cannot be built unless we drink the living water and remain attached to the anointed One. By drinking we receive the water, and by being attached we are under the anointing of the oil. By drinking we receive more life, and by being attached we receive more oil. By the water within and the oil without we daily grow and are built up. This is the practical building of the church. The church is built upon this rock.

We cannot be built with others or build others up by our own endeavor. Instead, we need to drink and remain attached to the anointed One. We all need to see a vision of the person of Christ and then declare what we see, saying, "Amen, this is Christ, the Son of the living God." Then we must go on to drink of the cleft rock in resurrection and to be attached to the anointed One. As a result, we shall be filled with water within and covered with oil without. This is the way we are built up.

THE LIFE AND THE OINTMENT FOR THE BUILDING

The Lord's great prophecy in Matthew 16:18 has not yet been fulfilled because most Christians are veiled and do not see that Christ today is the ointment and the life. They may know certain terms, but they do not have the revelation or the declaration. By making a declaration we testify that we have seen something. We have seen that Jesus, a wonderful person, is the Christ, the Son of the living God. He is the very embodiment of God, even God Himself. Furthermore, He is life and has the ointment. Everything God does is related to Him. Our Jesus is the Son of the living God, the embodiment of the divine substance, and He is now within us. When we receive this revelation, we can proclaim it to the universe. We also see that Christ has the ointment of God. All that God does, accomplishes, and intends is involved with Him. God within Him is life to us, and God upon Him is function to us. He has entered into us, and we have been attached to Him. Therefore, we have the life within and the function without. By declaring this we are built upon Him. In order for this building to continue, we need to drink of the water flowing in resurrection out of the cleft rock, and we need to remain attached to the anointed One and participate in the anointing. When we drink of the living flow, we receive nourishment for our growth. By remaining attached to the anointed One, we have ointment for our function. If we have both life and ointment, we shall grow and be built.

Matthew 16 mentions the Lord's crucifixion and resurrection. To be crucified means to be cleft, and to be resurrected means to flow out. The rock upon which the church is built had to be cleft so that the living water could flow out. The Lord was cleft, and in His resurrection the water flowed out. First Corinthians 15 deals with resurrection. In His resurrection Christ, the last Adam, became the life-giving Spirit. The last Adam was the cleft rock, and the life-giving Spirit is the living water flowing in His resurrection, flowing in the resurrected Christ. By drinking of the cleft and resurrected Christ, we receive the flowing water that enables us to grow and be built up.

I believe that Matthew 16:18 is now being fulfilled among us. The Lord has given us new light on the building of the church so that His prophecy might be fulfilled. I have the full assurance that many of us will see that Christ is the resurrected rock flowing with living water. After receiving such a revelation, many will spontaneously declare, "Amen, Lord Jesus. You are the Christ, the Son of the living God." By making this declaration, we receive more water within and more oil without. If we declare that Jesus is the Christ and the Son of the living God, we shall be filled with water and covered with oil. How blessed it is to be a Barjona who has seen the heavenly vision and has declared it! May we be beside ourselves with this revelation and proclaim it again and again. The more water and oil we receive, the more life and function we shall have. Then by life and function we shall become the corporate Christ, the one Body with the many members to fulfill God's purpose.

CHAPTER TWO

THE CONSTITUTION
OF THE CHURCH AND THE KINGDOM

Concerning God, there are two aspects: what God is and what God does. First, God is; second, He works and does certain things. Jesus of Nazareth came with these two aspects of God. However, He came first not to express what God is but to accomplish what God wanted Him to do for the fulfillment of His purpose. This means that Jesus came first not as the Son of God but as the Christ. For this reason, in Matthew 16:16 Peter said that Jesus was the Christ and then went on to say that He was also the Son of the living God.

THE IMPARTATION OF LIFE

Before we consider the function of the anointed One, we need to see that the Son of the living God is the embodiment of what God is. All that God is has been embodied in the Son. Therefore, the Son is the essence, the substance, of what God is. This is for life. The Father is the source of life, and the Son is the impartation of life. This means that the Father is the hidden One and that the Son is the expressed One. The Son is the expression of the Father to be the impartation of life. Therefore, if we have the Son, we have life. As 1 John 5:12 says, "He who has the Son has the life."

THE FUNCTION OF THE CHRIST

Now we need to see how the Son can be imparted into us as life. This is accomplished by the Christ. Perhaps you have never before realized that when the anointed One was crucified on the cross, He was carrying out His function. Daniel 9:26 says that the Messiah was to be cut off. His being cut off was

His function. As the anointed One was being cut off, He was functioning. Not only His death but also His resurrection and ascension were part of His function. Thus, the anointed One functioned by being crucified, by resurrecting, and by ascending so that the Son might be imparted into us as life. He is the Christ, the anointed One of God, to accomplish God's purpose. God's purpose is to impart what He is into us as life. This can be accomplished only by the function of the Christ, the anointed One of God. Through the function of the anointed One, the Son of the living God has been imparted into us, and we have life.

THE EXPERIENCE OF PETER

In Matthew 16 Peter received the revelation of the Christ and the Son of the living God. However, it was not until the day of resurrection that Peter received the Son of the living God into him as life. On that day the anointed One of God functioned through His crucifixion and resurrection to impart Himself as the Son of God into Peter. On the day of Pentecost the anointed One became Peter's experience. On the day of resurrection Peter received the Son of God as life; on the day of Pentecost he gained Christ for function. In other words, on the day of resurrection Peter became a son of God by receiving the Son of God. Then on the day of Pentecost Peter was anointed and became part of the anointed One, part of the corporate Christ.

THE CONSTITUTION OF THE CHURCH

The church is so many Barjonas, so many sons of natural fathers, who have received Christ as the Son of God and who have been attached to the anointed One. On the one hand, these Barjonas have the Son of God within them as life; on the other hand, they are attached to the anointed One to be part of the corporate Christ. This is the church.

In the past we have seen four aspects of the church: first, that it is the gathering of God's called ones; second, that it is the household, the family, of God; third, that it is the Body of Christ; and fourth, that it is the new man. However, no matter how clear we may be concerning these aspects of the church, we still need to know how the church is constituted. The church is constituted first with the Son of the living God and then with the Christ. Have you been constituted in this way, or are you still a Simon, a son of Jonah? Remember, on the day of resurrection Simon Barjona, the son of a natural man, was constituted with the Son of the living God. Thus, the Son of the living God was wrought into a man of blood and flesh. As the son of Jonah, Peter did not have the element of the Son of God. The Son of God was not a part of his constitution until the day of resurrection, when He was wrought into him through the death and resurrection of Christ. Therefore, in 1 Peter 1:3 Peter says that we were regenerated through the resurrection of Christ. Through Christ's resurrection Peter was constituted with the Son of the living God. A new element, a heavenly, divine element, was added to him. This was the first step.

The second step took place fifty days later. On the day of Pentecost, Peter was constituted further with the ascended Christ who came down upon him. On the day of resurrection the Son of God was wrought into him, and on the day of Pentecost the Christ was poured out upon him. Thus, by the day of Pentecost Peter was fully constituted with Christ within and without. From that time onward, he was no longer Simon or Barjona. He had become Peter, a stone.

The church is a group of sons of flesh and blood who have been constituted with the Son of God within and with the Christ without. Within we have life, and without we have function. Within we are full of living water, and without we are covered with oil. Thus, the church is a new constitution.

THE CHURCH AND THE KINGDOM

As we have seen, all that God is, is embodied in the Son, and all that God does is related to Christ, the anointed One. God's plan, His activity, and the accomplishment of His will are involved with Christ. Whatever God is—life, light, holiness, righteousness, love, kindness—is embodied in the Son. When we see the vision of this, we receive the Son and have life. We are also attached to Christ, the anointed One, and become part of the corporate Christ, the Body, the church. Such a church is the kingdom. The kingdom is composed of many transformed sons of Jonah. Simon was not a part of the kingdom, but Peter was. The son of flesh and blood is not part of the kingdom, but the son of the living God is. Are you a son of Jonah or a son of God? Are you part of Jonah or part of the anointed One? If you are a son of the living God and if you are a part of the anointed One, you are in the kingdom.

As the church, we are on the defensive, but as the kingdom, we are on the offensive. The Lord said, "Upon this rock I will build My church, and the gates of Hades shall not prevail against it" (Matt. 16:18). In this verse the gates of Hades are on the offensive, and the church is on the defensive. But when we are the kingdom, we are on the offensive, binding and loosing. Whenever we are sons of blood and flesh, we are food for Satan, for Satan eats the flesh. When we are sons of Jonah, we cannot shut the gates of Hades. But when we are Peters, not Simons, and are constituted with the Son of God and the Christ, we are no longer Satan's food. Rather, we are those who shut the gates of Hades and block the power of darkness. If we are the church against which the power of darkness cannot prevail, then we are the kingdom. Instead of waiting for the gates of Hades to attack us, we bind the gates and shut them. We are able to command Satan to flee. Today we are both the church and the kingdom.

THE KINGDOM AS THE TRANSFIGURATION OF JESUS

In Matthew 16:28 the Lord said, "Truly I say to you, There are some of those standing here who shall by no means taste death until they see the Son of Man coming in His kingdom." Then in 17:1 and 2 the Lord was transfigured on the mountain before Peter, James, and John. This indicates that His transfiguration was His coming in His kingdom. Before He was transfigured, there was no outward manifestation of the kingdom, because He was outwardly only a natural Nazarene. But when He was transfigured and entered into another realm, the realm of transfiguration, that realm became the kingdom. Hence, the kingdom is the transfiguration of Jesus.

We need to apply this principle to ourselves. When we are natural, we are sons of Jonah, not part of the kingdom. But when we are transformed into Peters, we have the keys of the kingdom, which were given not to Simon but to Peter. The keys of the kingdom were not given to the natural man, but to one who had been reconstituted and transformed. When Simon was transformed into Peter, he immediately received the keys of the kingdom.

RECONSTITUTED
THROUGH DEATH AND RESURRECTION

Prior to chapter 16 the Lord Jesus said nothing to His disciples about His crucifixion and resurrection. Only after they had seen Christ and the church, did He reveal His cross and resurrection to them. Apart from the crucifixion and resurrection of Christ, it is impossible for any son of Jonah to be reconstituted. Rather, every natural man would remain the same. A son of Jonah can be transformed and reconstituted only through the crucifixion and resurrection of Christ. Through death and resurrection Simon Barjona became Peter.

TRANSFERRED BY DRINKING

We need to understand how we are transferred from a son of Jonah to a Peter. As the rock, the Lord Jesus was cleft, and living water flowed out of Him. We have pointed out that the cleaving of the rock signifies the crucifixion of Christ and that the flowing out of the living water signifies His resurrection. When the Lord appeared to His disciples on the day of His resurrection, the mark of the cleft was still visible in His side (John 20:20). By Christ's being cleft, not only was the veil removed, but the living water was released. Living water is still flowing out of the Lord's side today. Today Christ is the life-giving Spirit in resurrection (1 Cor. 15:45). Because He is the Spirit, we can drink of Him. On the day we began to drink of Him, we were transferred from Simon to Peter. Moreover, by continuing to drink of Him we were solidly founded upon the rock, which is the crucified and resurrected Christ.

On the one hand, Christ is the flowing water; on the other hand, He is the rock. According to the principle of first mention, the significance of the rock in the Old Testament is the fact that it was cleft so that water could flow out. Eventually, this cleft rock flowing with water became the foundation stone for God's building. Today nearly all Christians know that Christ is the rock upon which the church is built and that He is the foundation of the church (1 Cor. 3:11). However, not many know the significance of Christ as the rock and the foundation. The significance is that the rock first was cleft so that the living water could flow out. Then as we drink of this flowing water, the cleft rock becomes our foundation, and we are solidly founded upon it. By drinking of the water from the cleft rock, we are transferred from Simon to Peter, and we are founded upon the crucified and resurrected Christ. Within us we have the flowing water, and beneath us we have the solid rock.

Being founded on the rock is not merely a matter of becoming a Christian and then coming together with other Christians. That is human organization. To repeat, Christ was cleft to flow out the essence of God as the living water to be our life. Today He is the cleft and resurrected Christ. When we see this vision, we respond to Him and drink Him in. I did this more than fifty years ago, although I did not know the meaning of what I had done. But as I recall my experience at the time I was saved, I realize now that I took a good drink of Christ and was watered within. Furthermore, I was transferred out of Simon into Peter. Although I was still muddy, the transfer had in fact taken place. Furthermore, at that time I became solidly founded upon the rock. Before I was saved, I was like a piece of driftwood. But after I received the Lord, I was founded on the cleft and flowing rock, on the crucified and resurrected Christ.

When we are transferred and founded, we become the church, and we are no longer food for Satan. Because our constitution has been changed, Satan can no longer eat us. If Satan tries to eat us, he will say, "Oh, I don't want to eat this! Once, you were so tasteful to me but not anymore." Many times I have said to Satan, "Satan, you don't want me, and I don't want you. I command you to leave." When this is our condition, we are not only the church on the defensive but also the kingdom on the offensive.

REACTING TO WHAT WE SEE

Are you a Simon or a Peter? If you are a Peter, then one day you saw the Christ, the Son of the living God, and you reacted to what you saw. You could not deny what you had seen. Some reacted by praying, others by crying, and still others by confessing how sinful they were. Our reaction depends upon what we see. Your reaction was your drinking of Christ. By drinking Him, you received Him. In other words, by your reaction, by your drinking, the Son of the living God came into you. He will never leave you, although there may be times when you think you want Him to leave. By our drinking of Him, the Son of the living God has been brought into our being, and we have been solidly founded upon the crucified and resurrected Christ. This is the constitution of the church. When we are such a church, we are spontaneously the kingdom.

The kingdom is both the transfiguration of Jesus and the transformation of so many sons of Jonah into Peters. All these sons of Jonah have been reconstituted to become not only the church on the defensive but also the kingdom on the offensive. The Lord was cleft in His crucifixion and flowed out the living water in His resurrection. When we saw this vision, we reacted to Him and drank Him in.

If you never see anything, you will not have any reactions. For example, as you drive along the highway, you react to the scenery. The aim of this ministry is to cause you to react. The more reaction, the better, for when you react, you drink. Every reaction is a drink that causes a further transfer and transformation. Some may not care whether or not they attend the meetings of the church. Those who stay home from the meetings are like those who never travel anywhere. Because they stay home, they see nothing new and hence have no reactions. We need to take a new way. Then we shall have one reaction after another. It does make a difference whether or not we come to the meetings, for in the meetings we will see things that cause us to react; and whenever we react, we drink. By drinking, we are transformed.

Have you seen that all that God is, is embodied in the Son? If you see this, you will react. Have you seen that all that God does is related to Christ, the anointed One? If you see this, you also will react. Have you seen that on the day of resurrection Peter received the Son of God and that on the day of

Pentecost he was attached to the anointed One? Anyone who sees this will have a strong reaction and be changed. After you have seen this, it will not be so easy for you to be the same as you were before. We need to have more reactions so that we may experience a further transfer from Simon to Peter. This transfer is for the church and the kingdom.

CHAPTER THREE

DENYING THE SELF
FOR THE BUILDING OF THE CHURCH

In Matthew 16:18 the Lord Jesus spoke of the gates of Hades, which signify the power of darkness. In the Bible Hades is the place of death, where people are held in the power of death. Hence, it is a region where death prevails. After the Lord Jesus died, He took a tour of Hades. Acts 2:24 indicates that Hades tried its best to hold Him. However, because Christ is the resurrection, He could not be held by death. Death cannot overcome resurrection; on the contrary, resurrection always subdues death.

THE GATES AND THE KEYS

The gates are mentioned in verse 18 of Matthew 16, and the keys in verse 19. The enemy has the gates, but we have the keys. The gates do not overcome the keys, but the keys control the gates. The enemy's gates are much bigger than the keys, but the gates are nonetheless under the control of the keys, just as the doors of a building are controlled by the keys that open and close them. Hallelujah, we have the keys! Satan has many gates, but we have the keys.

Now we need to consider what the keys of the kingdom are. Shortly after I was saved, I was taught by a great Bible teacher that the keys of the kingdom given to Peter were two in number. Peter used the first key to open the gate for the Jewish believers to enter the kingdom of the heavens on the day of Pentecost (Acts 2:38-42), and he used the other key to open the gate for the Gentile believers to enter the kingdom of the heavens in the house of Cornelius (10:34-48). I still believe that this teaching is correct. But, as we shall see, there is more to this matter of the keys than this.

In order to interpret the Bible, we must follow the basic principle of taking care of the context of every verse. In Matthew 16 Christ, the Son of the living God, the church, the kingdom, the gates of Hades, and the keys of the kingdom are all revealed. Verse 21 reveals what must take place for Peter to be transformed from a Simon to a Peter. For this, the Lord Jesus had to be crucified and resurrected. It was through the crucifixion and resurrection of Christ that Simon, the son of Jonah, became Peter, a son of God. Without this transaction it would have been impossible for Simon Barjona to become Peter.

THE LORD AS THE PATTERN AND THE PATHWAY

Verse 22 says, "Peter took Him aside and began to rebuke Him, saying, God be merciful to You, Lord! This shall by no means happen to You!" With a good heart Peter was telling the Lord that God should be merciful to Him. This verse is difficult to translate. Some say it should be rendered, "Lord, pity Yourself." According to this rendering, Peter was telling the Lord to be merciful to Himself. Another translation is, "God be merciful to You, Lord." It is difficult to determine the subject, whether it is God or the Lord Jesus. At any rate, the emphasis is on the self. Whether the subject is God or the Lord Jesus, the self is emphasized.

Verse 23 says, "But He turned and said to Peter, Get behind Me, Satan!" Then in verses 24 and 25 the Lord said to His disciples, "If anyone wants to come after Me, let him deny himself and take up his cross and follow Me. For whoever wants to save his soul-life shall lose it; but whoever loses his soul-life for My sake shall find it." According to these verses, the Lord is the pattern and the pathway. If anyone desires to come after Him, that is, take Him as the pattern and the pathway, he must deny himself, take up his cross, and follow Him.

SATAN COMING OUT THROUGH THE GATES

Verses 21 through 26 are necessary for the interpretation of verses 16 through 19. As we have seen, verse 18 speaks of the gates and verse 19 of the keys. In order to know what the gates and the keys are, we need to consider verses 21 through 26. Satan comes out through the gates. The first gate is the self. This means that we ourselves are one of the gates of Hades through which Satan comes out. Satan may come out through the gate of self even when we have a good heart. Whether our heart is good or evil, self is the first gate through which Satan comes out. In addition to the self, verses 21 through 26 also speak of the mind and the soul, both of which are also gates through which Satan comes out. Thus, the self, the soul, and the mind are the main gates through which Satan comes forth. Many times Satan has come out through your mind because your mind has been an open gate for him.

THE THREE KEYS

Verses 21 through 26 not only expose the gates but also reveal the keys. The first key is the denial of the self. Self is an open gate, but self-denial is the key that shuts it. The second key is the taking up of the cross. This means that the cross is a key to shut up the self, the soul, and the mind. The third key is the losing of the soul. Therefore, the three keys here are the denying of the self, the taking up of the cross, and the losing of the soul. Day by day we need to use these keys. Yes, Peter used the keys on the day of Pentecost and in the house of Cornelius. But we also need the three subjective keys found in this portion of the Word.

The principalities and powers in the heavenlies are gates. But in addition, the self, the soul, and the mind are three crucial subjective gates. If these subjective gates are locked, no principalities or powers will be able to come in.

THE CHURCH DAMAGED BY THE SELF

My burden in this chapter is not interpretation; it is application. Throughout history the church has not been damaged mainly by Judaism or Gnosticism; it has been damaged mainly by the self. Martin Luther once said that although he was afraid of the pope, he was more afraid of the stronger pope, the self, within his own heart. Nothing damages and frustrates the building up of the church more than the self. Self is the embodiment of the soul, which is expressed through the mind. Thus the self, the soul, and the mind are three-in-one. Behind these three is Satan, who manipulates the self in order to damage the church life. We all need to heed this word for ourselves.

Simply because of the self, certain saints have left the church life. In 1948 there was a certain brother in Shanghai who was full of self and whose soul was an open gate that no one could lock. He was ambitious to be an elder, and he often complained about the situation in the church. One day he stood up in a meeting to speak many negative things. After his negative speaking, I said, "Brother, there is no need for us to waste our time. If you can find a better place, please tell me about it, and I'll go there with you. But if you cannot find a better place, please be quiet and remain here." He had nothing more to say. A short while later, he stopped coming to the church meetings, began a meeting in his home, and hired a traveling preacher. With the financial support of this dissenting brother, this preacher wrote a long article opposing Brother Nee. No doubt, this brother damaged the church life. At the same time, he himself lost the church life. This was due to the self. With this brother there was no building, for he did not become a Peter but remained the son of Barjona. This was the result of Satan coming out through the self.

THE SERIOUSNESS OF BEING OFFENDED

Let me honestly and lovingly say a word to you all: It is a very serious matter to be offended. Do not casually say, "I have been offended in the church life. The elders and other leading ones have offended me." Although others may offend you, you will always be the first to suffer. On the one hand, I condemn all the offenses; but on the other hand, I must say that there is no excuse for your being offended. If we were not in ourselves, we could not be offended. If I exercise the key of self-denial to lock up the self, it will be impossible for me to be offended. The reason we are offended is that the self is so open and prevailing. Through the open gate of the self, Satan comes forth, and we are offended.

Perhaps in certain matters the church may be wrong. Do

not think that the church is no longer the church because it is wrong. For example, when your child makes a mistake, he is still your child. Whether the church is right or wrong, it is still the church. Although you may be offended by something or someone in the church, do not make any excuses for yourself. This frustrates the building up of the church.

USING THE KEY OF SELF-DENIAL

As we have seen, Matthew 16 speaks about the building up of the church and also about the gates of Hades and the keys of the kingdom. Without the keys to lock the gates, the church cannot be built. Because there has been so little exercise of these keys, the church has not yet been built. We may talk a great deal about the building. However, when certain things take place to touch us, the self is open. Because we are open to Hades, something from Hades—Satan—comes out. How we need to use the key of self-denial to lock the self! The way to keep from being offended by others is to lock up yourself by denying yourself. Blessed are those who are not offended.

There is no excuse for being offended. When the Lord Jesus comes and sets up His judgment seat, He will tell us to settle our account with Him. He may ask us why we were offended in certain places. But if we make excuses for ourselves, the Lord will not accept them. The problem is not the offense—it is the self. Certain viruses are very contagious. However, no virus can cause a table to be sick. If you can be offended, it is a proof that you are full of self. If my self has been locked up, I will not be offended no matter what you do to me or how you treat me.

NO NATURAL AFFECTION

I have spoken about being offended. Now I wish to say a word about natural affection. In the church life there should not be any natural friendships. If you regard certain ones as your special friends, it also is an indication that you are full of self. Certain ones match your taste, and you fit their taste. You feed one another's taste. This is very damaging, and it hinders the building. Among the brothers and sisters in the church, there should be a pure divine love, but there should not be any personal affection. If any personal affection creeps into your relationship with the saints, it proves that you are full of self. In the church life there should be no such affection. To me, all the brothers and sisters are the same. To have a favorite among the brothers and sisters is to be full of self. It is not to be a Peter but a son of Jonah. This damages the building.

We need to receive the mercy of the Lord to regard all the saints as our brothers and sisters but none as our friends. For the Lord's building in the church life, everything natural must be extracted. There should be no natural affection, relationship, or feeling. Rather, we all must be fearful of natural affection and shun it. Whenever a brother loves me in a naturally affectionate way, I am frightened. That is the time for me to exercise the key to deny the self. I will lock myself and avoid that brother's affection. Whenever you discover that you are feeding a brother's self and that he is feeding yours, you must use the key to lock the gate of the self. If you do not lock up the self, Satan will come out through the door of the self. Then you and others will remain sons of Jonah. You will not be Peters, and it will be impossible for the Lord to build the church with you.

THE HIDDEN SELF

More than nineteen hundred years ago, the Lord Jesus prophesied that He would build the church. But why, after so many centuries, do we not yet have the building? It is because the key of self-denial has been neglected. In these chapters I have no desire to talk about doctrines, but I do have a heart to fellowship with you all. Oh, the hidden self! Peter had a good heart, but within him there was the hidden self that became the gateway for Satan to come out. I appreciate the Lord's discernment. If I had been the Lord, I would not have had the discernment but would have appreciated Peter's concern. However, the Lord Jesus immediately discerned that Satan had come out through the gate of the self.

I am glad that in the churches we have the brothers' houses and the sisters' houses. But, through experience, we have realized that there are two kinds of results from living in such a house. Some form natural friendships; others become dissatisfied and disappointed. However, no matter what the situation may be, you should not be disappointed. To be disappointed is a proof that you are in the self. The self of those who live in the brothers' and sisters' houses must be locked up. If the self is locked up, we shall have the building. If you exercise the key of self-denial, others may be offended, but you will not be offended. Instead, you will be built up because the self in you has been locked up. We all need to use the prevailing key of self-denial to lock the self, the soul, and the mind. Otherwise, the building up of the church will be frustrated.

CRUCIFIED AND RESURRECTED
FOR THE BUILDING OF THE CHURCH

Verse 24 says, "If anyone wants to come after Me, let him deny himself and take up his cross and follow Me." The "Me" in this verse means a great deal. This "Me" is the pattern, the pathway. Furthermore, this "Me" is the crucified and resurrected "Me." If we are not crucified and resurrected, there can be no church. The church comes into existence through the crucifixion and resurrection of Christ. Not only our self, which is defiled, but even the Lord's pure, sinless self had to be denied. If the Lord had not denied Himself and gone to the cross, He could not have been resurrected, and there would have been no church. We must follow after Him. This means that we must deny ourselves as He did and must allow ourselves to be crucified as He did. Without this, it is impossible for the church to be built up. Whenever we sense that we are feeding the self-life of another, we must say, "Lord, I will follow You. I will stop having so much contact with this brother." If you do this, the building of the church will proceed.

KNOWING CHRIST, THE POWER OF HIS RESURRECTION,
AND THE FELLOWSHIP OF HIS SUFFERINGS

When you read this word, you may feel that you are not able to fulfill it. No, we cannot do it. This is why we need to pay attention to Paul's word in Philippians 3:10: "To know

Him and the power of His resurrection and the fellowship of His sufferings, being conformed to His death." Here we see that Paul desired to know three things: Christ, the power of His resurrection, and the fellowship of His sufferings. The "Him" in Philippians 3:10 is the "Me" in Matthew 16:24. We are not able to deny ourselves and go to the cross. But by the power of Christ's resurrection, we can do these things. Furthermore, through His resurrection we can enter into the fellowship of His sufferings and be conformed to His death. Although in ourselves we cannot do this, we have One living within us who can do it.

WORKING OUT OUR SALVATION

In Philippians 2:12 Paul says, "Work out your own salvation with fear and trembling." In the New Testament the word *salvation* is used in various ways. Regarding our eternal salvation, we cannot work anything out. The Lord Jesus has done everything to accomplish this. But we do need to work out the salvation that enables us to be built up together. For the building of the church, we need to work out this salvation.

The entire book of Philippians is a book on the building. Among the Philippians there was division and the lack of building. Thus, the apostle Paul wrote this Epistle to help them to be built up. Paul was telling them to work out the building, for this building was their salvation. Many Christians today are missing the building. This indicates that they are not working out their salvation.

Suppose you are living in the brothers' house. When you first moved in, you thought that living with the brothers would be wonderful. However, after a short period of time, you found that you could not get along with certain brothers. There is nothing you should do about this. Rather, remain in that brothers' house to be killed. Although you cannot suffer this killing, there is One in you who can. You simply need to follow Him to work out your salvation.

GOD WORKING IN US

Philippians 2:13 tells us how to work out our salvation: "It is God who operates in you both the willing and the working for His good pleasure." God is in us doing this work. We simply need to exercise the key of self-denial and say Amen to the Lord. We need to exercise the key to lock up the self. If we all learn this lesson, we shall be built up together, and we shall become a strong testimony. We shall be able to testify that although we have different characters, dispositions, temperaments, and backgrounds, we can be one and can be built up together. This is precisely what the Lord is dealing with in Matthew 16.

LOCKING UP THE SELF FOR THE BUILDING

Matthew 16 has been veiled for centuries. Perhaps you have read this chapter again and again and again without knowing what the Lord was really saying. But now the Lord has given us further understanding to see how the church can be built up through the exercise of the keys. We need to be afraid of ourselves and use the key to lock up ourselves. We should do this not only in the church life but also in our family life. If you exercise the key to lock up the self, you will have no problems in your marriage. All the problems are from Satan who comes out through the gate of the self. When this gate is locked, Satan is confined, and there are no problems.

In these chapters I am not concerned with mere doctrine. Instead, I am presenting to you what I have learned through years of suffering. We need to find out how the church can be built up. If you say that the church is built up through the cross and the resurrection, that is still too doctrinal. We need to go on to learn to exercise the key of self-denial to lock up the self in every situation. Whether a situation is for you or against you, you must lock up the self. Whether the brothers love you and welcome you or hate you and do not welcome you, you still need to lock up your self. If you do this, there will be no problems, and it will be possible to have the building of the church. But without the locking up of the self, there is no possibility of having the building.

主阿 保 训练我

让你训. 说话
让我练. 我给你..
比恺美你.

我不能长. 因为我在里嘟
所以给我光. 给我生命.
this rock 我们争夺最后的
王职分
让我的耳朵要动让.
不让我耳朵听假鹰.

不让我在对恃辩中.
让我在生命中

the way to build the church is to die
and to be in resurrection.

Chapter Four

BEARING THE CROSS
FOR THE BUILDING OF THE CHURCH

In the Gospel of Matthew various points are put together to reveal a doctrine. This is what Matthew did in chapter 16. After giving the revelation concerning Christ and the church, he unveiled the way the church is built.

THE WAY TO BUILD UP THE CHURCH

In Matthew 16:18 the Lord Jesus said, "I also say to you that you are Peter, and upon this rock I will build My church, and the gates of Hades shall not prevail against it." How can the church be built up in a practical way? The answer is found in verses 21 through 26. According to biblical terms, the way to build up the church is to be crucified and resurrected. Unless Christ had been crucified and resurrected, He could not build up the church. The church came into existence through His death and resurrection. Verse 21 says, "From that time Jesus began to show to His disciples that He must go to Jerusalem and suffer many things from the elders and chief priests and scribes and be killed and on the third day be raised." This verse indicates that the way to build up the church is through death and resurrection. On the mount the Lord Jesus was transfigured. This transfiguration, however, was temporary. Through death and resurrection Christ was permanently transfigured. Resurrection is a form of transfiguration. Through death and resurrection Christ has entered into a realm of transfiguration. The church exists in this realm of transfiguration. It cannot exist in the natural life or with fleshly people. It can exist only in a realm of transfiguration. As long as we are in a natural realm or in a fleshly condition, we are through with the church.

PETER'S DISSENSION

In verse 21 the Lord revealed the way to build the church. However, the one to whom He had given the keys of the kingdom did not agree with this way. When the Lord spoke to Peter regarding death and resurrection, Peter dissented and rebuked Him. Verse 22 says, "Peter took Him aside and began to rebuke Him, saying, God be merciful to You, Lord! This shall by no means happen to You!" But if this had not happened to the Lord, the church could have by no means been built up. If Peter, the one who received the keys, could be so dissenting, then any of us can be dissenting also. The history of Christianity is a history of dissension. The source of this dissension is Satan who comes out from Hades through the self. When the gate of self is open, Satan comes out to dissent.

When Peter rebuked the Lord, he was one with Satan. For this reason, verse 23 says, "He turned and said to Peter, Get behind Me, Satan! You are a stumbling block to Me, for you are not setting your mind on the things of God, but on the things of men." Here we see that Peter and Satan were one. Thus, the Lord rebuked Peter by calling him Satan and saying that he was a stumbling block to Him. The Lord also pointed out that Peter was not setting his mind on the things of God, but on the things of men.

TAKING UP THE CROSS

Verse 24 says, "Then Jesus said to His disciples, If anyone wants to come after Me, let him deny himself and take up his cross and follow Me." The Lord Jesus did not say to deny Satan but to deny the self. *Satan* and *self* are synonymous terms used interchangeably by the Lord. To deny the self is negative. In this chapter we need to see something on the positive side. The positive side is the matter of taking up the cross and following the Lord. We all have our cross. The Lord's cross is unique, but our crosses are many. In order for the church to be built, the Lord Jesus had to take up His cross, and we also must take up our cross.

Throughout the years this matter of taking up the cross and bearing the cross has been grossly misunderstood. For example, a brother who has lost a great deal of money in business may say that he must bear the cross. The book *The Imitation of Christ,* supposedly written by Thomas à Kempis, has been a help to many Christians. Nevertheless, that book contains an error: the concept that our human sufferings should be regarded as bearing the cross. This concept is very much like Hinduism. This is also a pronounced weakness of today's Catholicism, which emphasizes our need to suffer. Thus, the concept of suffering has crept into the Christian religion. In her biography Madame Guyon says that she even asked for crosses. This comes from the natural concept.

THE MEANING OF THE CROSS

We need to know the genuine meaning of the cross. Yes, the cross is a matter of suffering. Crucifixion was the method used by the Roman government to execute criminals. No doubt, to the criminal the cross was a suffering because he did not choose to be crucified. On the contrary, he was forced to be crucified. The crucifixion of the Lord Jesus, however, was altogether different. He was not forced to suffer crucifixion; He chose it. This was His own preference. He was not compelled to go to the cross; He was willing to do so because His cross was God's will. Hence, His crucifixion was for the fulfillment of God's will. The Lord was willing to take up the cross and be crucified for the fulfillment of God's purpose. In other words, Christ was not forced to die like a criminal. Rather, He was willing to be crucified so that through death His life might be released to produce the church. *Only things that went through the cross can build the church. Do we want to*

No doubt, the cross was a great suffering to the Lord, but *build the* He had no thought of reducing the suffering. Rather, when He *the church* was offered the wine mingled with gall, He rejected it (27:34; *or do we* Mark 15:23). The Lord did not care for the suffering; He cared *want other.* for the fulfillment of God's purpose. When He was on the cross, *to build the* the Lord suffered greatly. But that suffering was not forced *church?* upon Him. He took it willingly. In Matthew 26:39 the Lord prayed to the Father, "Not as I will, but as You will." At that same time He also prayed, "Your will be done" (v. 42). The Lord was willing to take up the cross, to go to the cross, and to remain on the cross until God's will had been fulfilled. This is the significance of the first mention of the cross in the Bible.

Confess (strict to the self. howly peace with other)

把 Christ 献给别人. 把平细它是给别.

NOT CRIMINALS
BUT WILLING BEARERS OF THE CROSS

According to this principle of first mention, all the other crosses must be the same as the first cross. This means that we are not forced to bear the cross but that we willingly take it up. Notice, the Lord Jesus did not say, "Let him deny himself and be crucified." No, He said, "Let him...take up his cross." We are not to be crucified, but we are to pick up the cross. However, certain brothers have said, "I have been crucified by my dear wife many times." Such brothers are not cross-bearers; they are criminals executed by their wives. If you say that your children are crucifying you, you are not a cross-bearer but an executed criminal. Today most Christians are criminals being executed; very few are cross-bearers. Let me ask you this question: Are you a criminal or a cross-bearer? We all need to say, "Praise the Lord, I am not a criminal. I am one who is willing to bear the cross. I have not been crucified by others; rather, I take up the cross and bear it."

OUR TURN TO TAKE UP THE CROSS

We have seen that the Lord did not suffer as a criminal but that He willingly took up His cross. He was a willing and happy cross-bearer for the purpose of fulfilling God's will to produce the church. Through His death His divine life was released to us, making us the members of the church. Today the problem is not with Him; it is with us. Although we have the divine life within us and have become members of the church, the problem is whether or not we shall be built up. We all have the divine life in us for the church, but we have not yet been built together. Throughout the centuries Christians have had the divine life in them for the church, but there has not been the building. Instead, there has been dissension, division, and confusion. Where is the building? Christ has done His best. Now it is our turn to take up the cross.

THE CROSS BEING GOD'S WILL

To take up the cross simply means to take up God's will. The cross is actually God's will. Anything that is not God's will is not a cross. The cross experienced by Christ definitely was God's will. If God's will had been that Christ should not die on the cross, yet Christ still went there and died, He would have been acting contrary to God's will. In such a case, that would not have been a cross but the execution of a criminal. However, the cross through which the Lord Jesus passed was not a criminal execution but the will of God.

According to God's ordination in the Bible, there is one husband for one wife. Consider how Abraham obtained a wife for his son Isaac. Before Abraham's servant brought Rebekah to Isaac, Isaac had never seen her. But when she was brought to him, he took her as his wife. This indicates that marriage, by whatever means it takes place, is sovereignly under the hand of God. Once you have married a certain one, she is your wife, and there is nothing more you can do about it. According to God's ordination, there must be no divorce. One husband for one wife is God's will. If you divorce your wife, you divorce your-self from God's will. But if you accept her, you accept God's will, because she represents God's will and even is His will. God's will is always a cross. However, if you suffer your wife as a cross, you are a criminal. But if you willingly take her by the Lord's grace, you are a cross-bearer. You willingly take up the cross; you are not executed. You recognize that your wife is God's will and ordination.

Suppose a brother's wife causes him to suffer. Since no divorce is permitted, he has two choices regarding her. He may either suffer with her like a criminal being executed on the cross, or he may take her as God's will and as his lot and por-tion. He may say, "God has allotted her to me. It was not I who married her; it was God who gave her to me. This is God's will, God's ordination. Hallelujah, I am willing and happy to bear the cross! I am not a criminal but a happy cross-bearer." If we do this, the presence of the Lord will be with us, and we shall enjoy the riches of life. Furthermore, we shall have a strong testimony of being built into one. *Anything that's not God's will, that is not the happy cross bearer.*

THE CHURCH BEING GOD'S WILL *Cross.*

We may apply the same principle to the church life. In the universe there is just one church, and in any locality there should also be one church. The one church is God's ordination

If you suffer her, you're a criminal. 忍受她   你连喜欢 or 不喜欢
If you by grace, the indwelling grace, you're not executed. 她都是你的事.

and allotment. This is His portion to us, and this is His will. Whether we like the church or not does not mean anything, because the church is God's will. Perhaps at first you were very happy with the church, and you enjoyed a church-life honeymoon. But later you came to dislike the church and desired a separation from it. Many Christians today have divorced themselves from the church. But if we do this, we neglect Matthew 16. If we can divorce the church, there will be no building. Through the centuries many Christians have been like a woman who has had several husbands. After staying with a certain man for a period of time, she divorces him in order to be with another man. This is the actual situation among today's Christians. We need to recognize that the one church is God's will and ordination and that we have no choice about it. Therefore, eventually the church becomes the cross that we must bear. The question is whether we shall bear it like a criminal being executed or bear it willingly and happily. We should be like Christ who made the cross His choice, His first preference. Although being in the church may cause us difficulties, there is nothing we can do about it, for the church is the church. Thus, we all need to pray, "Lord, grant me the sufficient grace to make me a willing cross-bearer." If you pray like this, you will become a happy bearer of the cross, not a criminal. As a result, you will have the genuine building.

Nearly all Christians today choose a church according to their taste, like people who choose restaurants according to their taste. Some may not like a certain church because the members shout and call on the name of the Lord. Others prefer a church where they can speak in tongues or hear musical performances by soloists, quartets, and choirs. If we are like this, then there is no bearing of the cross. First, we must find out what the church is. Once we find out, there must be no further preference, no further choice. Whether we like the church or not, we must recognize that the church is not according to our taste but according to God's will and ordination. We simply need to claim the sufficient grace that we may become a happy bearer of the cross. We need to say, "Lord, make me a willing cross-bearer like You were. You learned what God's will was in Matthew 26, and then You were willing to do it. You were glad to take up the cross. You could have summoned twelve legions of angels to rescue You, but You did not do it. You were willing to bear the cross. Thank You, Lord, that through Your willingness to bear the cross we are here today as the church. Now, Lord, we want to partake of Your willingness to take up the cross so that Your life may be released." *Your willingness → Your life is released*

THE BROTHERS AND SISTERS BEING GOD'S WILL
my willingness → my life is released

Not only is the church God's will, but every brother and sister in the church is also His will. According to the Bible, we have no way to divide ourselves from the brothers and sisters. If we prefer certain brothers and sisters above others, we are a Barjona, a son of flesh and blood. In the church every brother and sister is God's will, and we have no choice regarding them. The Father has begotten them all, and we need to accept them all as His will. There is no room for our likes or dislikes, both of which are natural. In the church there are no special friendships and no preferences. Thus, eventually every brother and sister becomes a cross to us. However, if we receive mercy and grace from the Lord, we shall become a happy bearer of the cross, not a criminal condemned to execution. *Drop the*

If I say that I do not like a certain brother and will no *cross* longer spend any time with him, I spontaneously stop bearing *↓* the cross. As soon as I forsake the cross, the building ceases. *No building* The church has not been built over the past nineteen centuries because not many have been willing to take up the cross. Are you willing to bear the cross? The whole church, with every brother and sister in it, is a cross. We have no choice, no preference. We must bear the church and we must bear all of the saints, whether we like them or not. If we have our preference, we are not bearing the cross, and there can be no building. Wherever I am, I have no choice, for there is just one church. *Good. bad. none. Praise Him for putting us together. [No like. No dislikes].*

DEALING WITH OUR TASTE

Some saints in the Lord's recovery, however, have tried to have their choice regarding the church. After staying in a certain place for a period of time, they became unhappy with the church there, especially with the leading ones. Therefore, they moved to another locality and stayed there for another period of time. Being unhappy there, they moved to still another place. In each locality the situation was the same. This illustrates the fact that no church can satisfy you according to your taste. Instead, what you need to do is to willingly bear the cross. Do not make any selection, for all the churches are the same. If you cannot be happy in one place, you will not be happy in any other place. Do not try to deal with the church, but deal with your taste.

NO PREFERENCES

Our preference & choice fluctuate

Many are able to get along with the church but not with some of the saints. If this is your situation, you are finished with the building. We need to take up the cross. If you make a selection among the churches, you are a wide open gate for Satan to come out. Thus, you must use the second key—the taking up of the cross. We need to say, "Lord, Your will is that there be one church in the universe and one church in every city. Lord, Your will is also that I be one with all my brothers and sisters. As long as anyone is a believer, I must accept him without choice or preference. My likes or dislikes do not mean anything." This is the unique way for us to be built together. Otherwise, our preferences and tastes will constantly fluctuate. Today I may feel positively toward you, but tomorrow I may feel negatively. Both in the church life and in married life there should be no fluctuation. What can keep us stable and steadfast is the bearing of the cross. This is the second practical key for the building of the church.

In the previous chapter we saw that the first key is denying the self. Now we see that the second key is taking up the cross. Denying the self is negative, whereas taking up the cross is positive. The only way to fulfill God's will is to take up the cross. Do not blame the brothers and sisters, and do not even blame yourself. Rather, simply take up the cross. Do not give any ground to your choice or preference. Your destiny is God's will, God's ordination. We need to take the one church and all the brothers and sisters as God's will. However, deep within us we may have certain preferences. We may like some and dislike others. Because we are natural and human, we all have our preferences. But if we exercise our preference, there will not be any building.

A TESTIMONY OF THE GENUINE ONENESS

All the demons and evil angels are observing us and examining our testimony. Thus, our testimony is not merely before men but before the whole universe. What a shame it is if we talk about the building but do not actually have the building because of our natural preferences! We need to pray, "Lord, help us and grant us the sufficient grace. We want to bear the cross so that no evil angel may be able to say a negative word about our testimony. We are here as the testimony of the building, and we want there to be no ground for the demons and evil angels to say anything." Man may not know what is taking place, but all the demons and evil angels understand what we are doing. They know what is in our heart and whether or not we are willing to take up the cross. If we are willing to bear the cross, then we are a real testimony.

A battle is raging today not simply before men but before all the evil powers. Thus, we must have no preferences, no choices, except the will of God; and we must take up the cross, that is, take up the will of God. If we have seen the vision of the one church and of all the saints as the members of the one Body, then we shall have no choice and no personal taste. We should not care for our taste, feeling, or consciousness. Rather, we should care only for God's will that we would have the genuine oneness, the oneness that can stand the investigation of all the demons and the principalities and powers. We want to have the testimony before the evil powers that we are a people with the genuine oneness because we are all willing to take up the cross. We are not suffering like criminals, but we are happy cross-bearers. I believe that at this end time throughout the entire earth there will be a people bearing such a testimony.

CHAPTER FIVE

LOSING THE SOUL
FOR THE BUILDING OF THE CHURCH

Nearly all Christian teachers have isolated Matthew 16:21-28 from verses 16 through 19 of the same chapter. They have regarded verses 16 through 19 as a section concerning Christ, the church, and the kingdom. To my knowledge, no one has connected these verses to the following verses. Because of this, many have been veiled from seeing the fact that verses 21 through 28 disclose the way to build the church. Years ago we saw the revelation concerning Christ and the church and the prophecy that Christ would build His church. However, until recently, we did not see the way to build the church. In verses 21 through 26 we have the keys to realize the building of the church. The practical and definite way for the church to be built up among us is found in these verses.

THE THREE KEYS

In these verses we have not only the death and resurrection of Christ but also three keys that we need to exercise: the denial of the self, the bearing of the cross, and the losing of the soul-life. If we use these three keys, we are immediately and spontaneously on the way to the building of the church. In the past we did not have the definite and practical way to build the church. But now we have seen the three keys. We need to deny the self, take up the cross, and lose the soul-life. As we have pointed out, to take up the cross is not a matter of suffering but of accepting the will of God. It is to accept the church and every believer as God's will. Every believer in Christ is God's will for you. Furthermore, the church is the will of God. Thus, both the church and all the believers are a

Every believer and the church are the cross that we need to take.

cross to us. We need to take up this cross and bear it. In the foregoing chapters we have considered the first two keys. In this chapter we shall consider the third key.

THE SOUL AND THE SOUL-LIFE

Verse 25 says, "For whoever wants to save his soul-life shall lose it; but whoever loses his soul-life for My sake shall find it." This verse begins with the word *For,* indicating that it is an explanation of the previous verses. The Greek word rendered "soul-life" or "life" (KJV) is *psuche,* the word for *soul.* Although it is correct to render this word as "soul-life," it can also be rendered "soul." Actually, this translation is preferable here. Rendered this way, verse 25 speaks of the saving and the losing of the soul. There is a difference between the soul and the soul-life. The soul is our natural being, whereas the soul-life is our human life. These two are inseparable.

THE SOUL AND THE SELF

Luke 9:25 says, "For what is a man profited if he gains the whole world but loses or forfeits himself?" This verse does not speak of the soul or the soul-life but of the self. When this verse is compared with Matthew 16:26, we see that the soul is the self and that the self is the soul. However, there is still a difference between the soul and the self. According to the context of Matthew 16, the self in verse 24 is the embodiment and expression of the soul in verse 25. Moreover, the expression of the self is mainly through the mind. For this reason, verse 23 speaks of setting the mind on the things of men, not on the things of God. Therefore, in verses 23, 24, and 25 respectively, we have the mind, the self, and the soul. The soul is embodied in the self, and the self is expressed through the mind.

In verse 25 the word *soul* indicates enjoyment. If you consider the context of verses 25 through 27, you will see that the Lord was speaking about the enjoyment of the soul. To save the soul is to allow the soul to have its enjoyment. Thus, the self is the expression of the soul, and the soul itself is the enjoyment. To lose the soul means to lose the enjoyment of the soul, and to gain the soul means to have the enjoyment of the soul.

SOULISH ENJOYMENT

As tripartite men, we have three kinds of enjoyment: physical enjoyment, spiritual enjoyment, and psychological enjoyment. Physical enjoyment includes the enjoyment of fine food and of a pleasant place to rest. Spiritual enjoyment includes the enjoyment of God's presence, God's blessing, God's speaking, and God's grace. Between the physical enjoyment and the spiritual enjoyment there is the psychological enjoyment, which includes things such as the enjoyment of sweet music, the satisfaction of being praised by others, and the pleasure of being with our intimate friends.

Which of these three types of enjoyment do you think is the highest? According to the New Testament, both the physical enjoyment and the spiritual enjoyment are for the soulish enjoyment. The reason for this is that God did not create man as a body or as a spirit but as a soul. In Matthew 11:29 the Lord Jesus said that if we would take His yoke upon us and learn from Him, we would find rest for our souls. This kind of rest, however, needs to be supported by the rest of the spirit. If our spirit does not rest in the Lord, our soul cannot be at rest. Soulish rest needs to be supported by spiritual rest. Those who attend nightclubs may be satisfied in a fleshly, soulish way, but they do not have the support of spiritual satisfaction. Because they lack this support, their fleshly and sinful satisfaction is vain. However, the rest we enjoy in our soul is lasting because it has the support of the rest in the spirit, the support of spiritual satisfaction.

The highest enjoyment is neither the physical nor the spiritual but the soulish. The physical enjoyment is for the soulish enjoyment, and the spiritual enjoyment supports the soulish enjoyment. As human beings, we all seek enjoyment. There is no one on earth who does not seek it. Even children desire enjoyment. The children's enjoyment is mainly in their soul. Soulish enjoyment dominates their actions and behavior. The behavior of children is genuine because with them there is no performing. But as we grow up, our behavior ceases to be genuine because we learn to perform. Genuine enjoyment is soulish enjoyment. Therefore, what the Lord was talking about in Matthew 16 was the soulish enjoyment.

THE REWARDS FOR LOSING OR SAVING THE SOUL

The Lord said that whoever desires to save his soul will lose it, and that whoever loses his soul for His sake will find it. For both the losing of the soul and the saving of the soul we shall be rewarded. Matthew 16:27 says, "The Son of Man is to come in the glory of His Father with His angels, and then He will repay each man according to his doings." If we deny the self, take up the cross, and lose the soul, we shall receive one kind of reward. But, if we save the soul, we shall receive a different kind of reward. One way or another, at the time of the Lord's coming, we shall be rewarded.

This reward, however, is not strictly a matter of the future. This is proved by verse 28: "Truly I say to you, There are some of those standing here who shall by no means taste death until they see the Son of Man coming in His kingdom." The Lord will come in two ways, in His coming in the future and in His coming in His transfiguration. The Lord's transfiguration on the mountain was a form of the coming of the kingdom. In both types of comings there is a reward according to our doings, according to whether or not we deny ourselves, take up the cross, and lose the soul.

SAVING THE SOUL BEING TO PLEASE THE SELF

We need to understand this matter of the saving or losing of the soul in the light of our experience. We also need to remember that the subject of the last half of Matthew 16 is the building of the church, and that we should not isolate verses 21 through 28 from verses 16 through 19 since these verses are concerned with the way to build up the church. Suppose the brothers living in a brothers' house have seen the vision concerning Christ and the building of the church. They realize that the Lord desires to recover the church life for His economy. However, the living situation in the house may not be very encouraging. Perhaps no one is willing to do the dishes. Because of the discouraging situation, some of the brothers may consider moving out of the house. But if they move out, they will be saving their souls to have an easy way for themselves. One brother may actually move from that house to another house, where, after a few weeks, he learns that the situation is the same. Then he moves to a church in another part of the country, concealing the reason for his move under the cloak of seeking a better church life. By making this move, he is saving his soul. When he arrives in the new locality and moves into a brothers' house there, he finds the situation even worse than the one he left. At this point, disappointed with the church life, he may decide to leave the church entirely. If he does this, he will be saving his soul to the uttermost. By this we see that to please the self is to save the soul.

USING THE THIRD KEY

The more logical a person is, loves the physical enjoyment more.

Now we need to see what it means to lose the soul. In the process of the building of the church, we should not save our soul. Rather, we must always lose it. Do not move from one brothers' house to another to seek a better situation to make things easier for yourself. Every brother is God's will, and you need to bear each brother as a cross. If others will not wash the dishes, then you should wash them. But if you feel sorry for yourself because you are the only one to wash the dishes, the gate will be opened for Satan to come forth. He will tempt you to move out of the brothers' house. When such a temptation comes, you need to use the third key, the key of losing the soul. If you use this key, you will say, "Praise the Lord! Tomorrow I shall wash even more dishes. Satan, don't talk to me anymore. The more you talk to me, the more dishes I will wash. I am willing to lose my soul to the uttermost." After a short period of time of losing the soul, there will be a transfiguration in the church, and in this transfiguration you will be rewarded positively. In the church life and in all the meetings you will have the highest enjoyment of the Lord's presence. But those who have been saving their soul will be rewarded negatively during this time of transfiguration. 主所有. 你知道我们必. 平也是很.

The Lord's interest today is with the building of the church. But how can we, as fallen human beings, be built up together? It is difficult even for a husband and wife or for parents and children to be built up together. We all want enjoyment for ourselves and react against anything that touches our sense of enjoyment. Apart from the losing of the soul, it is impossible for the church to be built up. If someone offends you, you may be unwilling to forgive him simply because you enjoy being able to condemn him. Because forgiving him is not enjoyable to you, you have no interest in forgiving him. This is true not only in the church but also between husbands and wives. Sisters, once your husband has offended you, you may enjoy holding on to that offense. Holding on to it and refusing to forgive him affords you psychological pleasure. This is the saving of the soul. If you save your soul in this way, you cannot have a proper family life. In order to have a proper family life, we need to lose our soul. Our soulish enjoyment must go. If you are willing to lose your soulish enjoyment, you will be rewarded one day when the Lord comes into your family. At that time, the Lord will save your soul. You were willing to lose it, but when the Lord comes in, He will save it and cause you to have great enjoyment. For the building of the church there is the crucial need that we all learn to lose our soul. Do not keep any enjoyment for your soul. Rather, lose it for the Lord's sake.

NOT A SUFFERING BUT A JOY

With respect to the losing of the soul, the Lord did not speak about suffering. Do not think that if you lose the soul, you will suffer. If you have had some experience with this matter, you will know that apparently the losing of the soul is a suffering, but actually it is a real joy. If a sister loses her soul by forgiving her husband, that will be a joy to her and to her family. It will issue in the building up of the proper family life. The same is true in principle with the building of the church. To lose our soulish enjoyment is a joy because as a result we see the building up of the church. If you are willing to lose your soul in a practical way, others will be nourished by you and built up through you. This is not a suffering; it is a joy.

Hebrews 12:2 says that the Lord endured the cross because of the joy that was set before Him. The Lord did not go to the cross with tears; rather, He went joyfully. His going to the cross was His losing of His soul. But because He foresaw the result, He did not feel sorry for Himself about losing His soul. He knew that through His death many grains would be brought forth (John 12:24).

The need today is that we all learn how to lose our soul. In the church life do not insist on preserving any soulish enjoyment for yourself. This does not mean, however, that those in the brothers' houses are expected to work like slaves. The parents of some of the brothers may misunderstand this. If you have the grace, you will realize that the losing of the soul is not a form of slavery. As you are washing dishes in the brothers' house, you will be happy and willing to lose your soulish enjoyment to satisfy others. *Ive don't insist. assist any soulish enjoyment in the church life.*

THE CHURCH TRANSFIGURED
THROUGH THE LOSING OF THE SOUL

To loose my joy for your joy. for the Lord's sake

The losing of the soul is the basic factor in our being built up together. It is not only a matter of denying the self or of bearing the cross but of losing the soul. We need to lose all our *for the church sake* present soulish enjoyment for the Lord's sake, for the sake of the church, and for the sake of all the saints. If you are willing to lose your soul for the sake of others, those with you will be enlightened, nourished, and filled. This is the way the church is built. If all the saints are willing to lose the soul, what a wonderful situation there will be among us. There will be no offenses and even no need for forgiveness. If we are like this, we shall be rewarded with a prevailing transfiguration. But if we are not willing to lose our soul, we shall not share in this transfiguration. On the contrary, for us the church life will be darkness, and, during the time of transfiguration, we shall be rewarded with suffering. Instead of being joyful, we shall be in darkness. This is a negative reward for being unwilling to lose the soul.

Our willingness to lose the soul for the Lord's sake will cause the church to be transfigured. In other words, it will bring in a revival. Every genuine revival is a coming of Christ, a present coming of Christ with His reward (not His second coming in a physical way). He rewards the faithful ones positively and the unfaithful ones negatively. I have seen this happen in the church life. When a revival, a transfiguration, came, some were enjoying and others were gnashing their teeth in darkness.

Wash and cleanse me.
May You chengsh and nourish Your people.

No opinion (denial of the self)

NO FEELING OF DISSENSION

The Lord appointed Bro in that position, we'll just follow

(that doesn't mean others' way is better)

Some time &
Some feelings of dissension.

How I thank the Lord for showing us these three keys, the keys of self-denial, bearing the cross, and losing the soul! If we deny ourselves, we shall not have any opinions. When I was working with Brother Nee in China, I realized that he had been appointed by the Lord to take the lead. Therefore, I did whatever he said. However, this did not mean that I did not sometimes have a better way to do certain things. According to my knowledge, my way would sometimes have saved a great deal of time. Nevertheless, I did not say a word, simply because I did not want Brother Nee to feel that I was dissenting with him. Instead of taking the time necessary to make my way clear, I denied myself, forgot my way, and followed Brother Nee's way. Actually, this not only saved time; it also saved us from the feeling of dissension. We all are human. If we say contrary things to one another, it is difficult to avoid the feeling of dissension. This feeling is subtle, and it may give rise to friction between us.

LEARNING TO BE FLEXIBLE

In 1934 Brother Nee conducted a conference in Hang-chow. At this conference I met a certain co-worker whom Brother Nee knew very well. Regarding him, Brother Nee said, "This brother is very good. Whenever you tell him to go west, he will go east." However, Brother Nee did not criticize this brother. At first, I did not understand Brother Nee's language, although his word impressed me. Eventually, I learned that this brother was exactly like Brother Nee had said. In those days we were all learning to deny the self. If we had insisted that this brother go in a certain direction, it would have meant that we were not denying ourselves. We had to deny ourselves to fit into his situation. We knew that if we told him to go west, he would go east. Therefore, if we wanted him to go west, we would suggest that he go east. Then he would go west.

Because similar situations exist among us today, all the elders need to learn to be flexible. They also need to become familiar with the various dispositions of the saints. The way to learn this is by denying the self. Although a brother may always act contrary to what we say, he is still a brother. He is the will of God for us, and we must deny the self and take him up as a cross. As we endeavor to do this, we also need to lose our soulish enjoyment.

LOSING THE SOUL IN THE FAMILY LIFE AND IN THE CHURCH LIFE

Husbands and wives argue with each other because they find it enjoyable. The reason a husband is not willing to lose the case to his wife is that it would mean the losing of his soul. But if a brother loses his soul by losing the case to his wife, the Lord will reward him by coming in at a certain point to save his soul. That will be the time for the soul to have its enjoyment. This illustrates the fact that the family life is built up through the losing of the soul. There cannot be a proper family life without the losing of the soul. For the sake of the family, you need to lose your enjoyment. Then the Lord Jesus will reward you in a positive way when He causes a transfiguration to take place in your family.

The same is true in the church life. In the church we all need to learn to lose our soul, to lose our soulish enjoyment. By losing our soul, a transfiguration will take place. Then in the Lord's transfiguration we shall be rewarded positively, and the Lord will save our soul. If you consider your experience, you will find that this is true.

Without the third key, the losing of the soul, the first two keys do not work very well. We need the last key, the losing of the soul, in the church life. In every aspect of the church life we need to lose our soul. If we lose our soulish enjoyment, we shall not argue with the brothers. Therefore, the losing of the soul is the way for the church to be built up. By the exercise of the three keys, the gates of Hades are locked up, and the doors of heaven are opened. When Hades is locked up and the heavens are opened, we shall have an excellent church life. This excellent church life is the kingdom today. This is the way for the church to be built up.

① Deny yourself.

② take up the cross

③ losing the soul life.

Church life = kingdom.

CHAPTER SIX

THE SALVATION OF THE SOUL

In this chapter we shall cover the matter of the salvation of the soul. James 1:21 speaks of the saving of the soul, and 1 Corinthians 5:5 speaks of the saving of the spirit. Other verses also mention the saving of the soul. For example, 1 Peter 1:9 says, "Receiving the end of your faith, the salvation of your souls." James 1:21 tells us to receive in meekness the implanted word, which is able to save our souls. Some Christians consider the saving of the spirit the same as the saving of the soul. However, according to the New Testament, our spirit and soul are two different things. First Thessalonians 5:23 reveals clearly that we are a tripartite man composed of spirit and soul and body. Thus, these three parts are distinct from one another.

THE THREE ASPECTS OF GOD'S SALVATION

Because man is a tripartite being, God's salvation revealed in the Bible is of three aspects. First, God saves our spirit by regeneration. Then He works to transform our soul so that our soul may be saved. Finally, Romans 8 says that our body will be redeemed, that is, transfigured. Therefore, God's salvation is a complete salvation for our entire being—spirit, soul, and body. With God's salvation there are three aspects—the aspects of the saving of our spirit, soul, and body.

Many Christians are clear that regeneration is the saving of the spirit. Furthermore, all genuine Christians believe that when the Lord Jesus comes back, our body will be changed. However, not many Christians have a clear understanding of the salvation of the soul or of the verses that refer to this matter (Matt. 16:25; Heb. 10:39; James 1:21). When I was young, I was troubled by these verses. I said to myself, "I have received

We need to eat, that we may supply all the needs of the body.

salvation already. Why must I wait to receive the salvation of the soul?" According to the New Testament, we all have received salvation in our spirit. When we believed in the Lord Jesus and were washed in His blood, we were regenerated by the Holy Spirit and saved. Although the salvation in our spirit is ours already, there is another kind of salvation, the salvation of our soul, for which we must wait until the Lord comes back. This salvation is not obtained merely by believing; it must be accomplished by the implanted word. The living word of God is implanted into our being to work out something. As the years have passed, the light has shone brighter and brighter on the matter of the saving of the soul, and we have been able to differentiate the three aspects of God's salvation corresponding to the three parts of our being. Man's spirit is deadened. For this, we need salvation in our spirit. Man's soul has been ruined. For this, we need salvation for our ruined soul. Furthermore, man's body has been corrupted and is subject to death. Hence, we need salvation for our corrupted and dying body.

RECEIVING AND DIGESTING GOD

The book of Genesis reveals that God created man with the purpose of expressing Himself through man. In order to fulfill this purpose, God created man with three parts, one of which is the human spirit, the organ by which we contact God and receive Him into us. Just as God created the stomach to receive and digest food, so He created our spirit to contact, receive, and even digest God. When the Lord Jesus, God incarnate, came, He said that He is the bread of life and that whoever eats Him shall live because of Him (John 6:48, 57). Thus, the very God incarnate likened Himself to our food supply. Food is not meant to be preserved in storage or in a refrigerator but to be taken in and digested by us. The fact that the Lord Jesus likened Himself to our food supply, the bread of life, indicates that we need to eat Him and digest Him. Are you troubled by the thought that man can digest God? Digesting God is a very positive thing, because God's intention is to work Himself into our being. The only way that something outside of us can be wrought into our being is through eating and digesting it.

Therefore, <u>God created us with a spirit as the organ</u> to receive <u>Him and digest Him</u>, that is, <u>to take Him as our life supply.</u>

John 4:24 says that <u>God is Spirit and that those who worship Him must worship Him in spirit.</u> This means that <u>we need to contact God.</u> When we contact Him, <u>He comes into us not only as our life but also as our life supply.</u> The Lord is both life and the bread of life. In John 11:25 the Lord said that He is life, and in John 6:48 He said that He is the bread of life. After we receive life, we must have the life supply. If a baby does not receive nourishment after it is born, it will die. First, Christ becomes our life. Immediately after this, the very Christ who is our life becomes our life supply. This is not a matter in our mind but in our spirit.

EXPRESSING THE SUBJECTIVE GOD

Christ is our life and life supply for the purpose that we might express God. God cannot be expressed through man in an objective way. If He would remain in heaven and not get into us and be wrought into our being, He could not be expressed through us. <u>God had to find a way to enter into us and to be wrought into us</u> so that our being would <u>express not ourselves but God.</u> Therefore, the objective God, the God far away from us, has become the subjective God in our very being. He is not only within us but is being wrought into us. Therefore, the apostle Paul could say, "To me, <u>to live is Christ</u>" (Phil. 1:21). Paul did not say, "To me, to live is Saul of Tarsus, a learned Jew." He said, "To me, to live is Christ," because <u>the very God in Christ had been received by Paul</u> and <u>wrought into his being.</u> Paul did not express himself, but Christ who had been wrought into him. This is God's purpose, and it is the reason He created us with a spirit and a soul. *we live out what we eat.*

According to the Bible, our soul is our being, our character, our person. As persons, we are not intended by God to express ourselves. Rather, God intends that we express Him. In our <u>daily life</u> and in our <u>behavior</u> we should not express ourselves but God. In order to express God, we (first) need to exercise our <u>spirit and take Him into us.</u> Then we need to live the kind of life in our being, person, and character that expresses Him. Then people will say, "This person does not express the American way of life; he expresses God." For us to receive God, we need a spirit; and for us to live Him out and express Him, we need a personality, which is our soul.

Some may think that those who are strong can express God but that those who are not so strong cannot express Him. Others think that the intelligent ones can express God but that the dull ones cannot. However, the dull ones often can express God better than the intelligent ones. I have known a number of intelligent believers who did not express God; instead, they expressed their cleverness. But I have also known some country people with very little education who truly expressed God because they lived by God and expressed Him through their personality.

We have seen that we have a spirit to receive God and a soul to live out God. Perhaps you are wondering what the function of our body is. Without a body we would be a phantom. As human beings, we need a tangible physical body. Having such a body, we are normal. Therefore, God created us with a spirit to take Him in, a soul to express Him, and a body to contain ourselves in a normal way. For His purpose, God had to create us with these three parts.

MAN'S FIRST SIN

In Genesis 1 we see God's creation, and in Genesis 2 we see clearly that God's intention in creating man was that man would receive Him as the tree of life. But in Genesis 3 the tempter came in to stir up the enjoyment of the soul, tempting Eve with the fruit that would make her like God. The aim of this temptation was to arouse the soul. When the soul is selfish, it becomes the self. It is altogether right to have a soul. But when the soul desires something for itself, it becomes selfish. The soul was created by God for the purpose of expressing Him, not to have its own enjoyment or preferences. Brother Nee put out a book entitled *The First Sin of Man*. Man's first sin was not adultery, stealing, or murder; it was taking something according to his own preference. To take fruit was not wrong, but to take fruit according to the preference of the soul was the activity of the self. Therefore, man's first sin was to do something for himself, to satisfy the self.

To repeat, the soul was made to express God. But when the soul does something to satisfy itself, it becomes selfish. This is the reason we must deny ourselves. To deny ourselves means to reject the soul's desire, preference, and choice. Whenever the soul wants something for itself, we must deny the soul. The desire of the soul for something for its own satisfaction was the cause of man's fall. By taking the fruit of the tree of the knowledge of good and evil, man fell, and his soul was ruined. The soul created by God for the purpose of expressing God had been ruined by the desire of the self. Because of this, the spirit lost its function, having become defiled and deadened. Furthermore, the body entered into death. This is a complete picture of fallen man: the soul ruined, the spirit deadened, and the body subject to death.

RECEIVING THE SALVATION OF THE SPIRIT

Because we are in such a fallen condition, we need God's salvation. Thank the Lord that He has come in to be our Savior. He put our nature on Himself and became the Lamb of God, who took away the sin of the world (John 1:29). Through His redemption our sins have been forgiven. Now God has a way to contact us and to bring us into His presence. We have been called, we have repented, we have believed in the Lord Jesus, we have been cleansed, and the Spirit of God has come into our spirit. Thus, we have been reborn, and our deadened spirit has been made alive. This is the salvation of the spirit.

Once we have received this salvation, we shall never lose it. This is proved by 1 Corinthians 5:5, a verse that speaks of a sinful brother. Although this one had been regenerated, he fell into a terrible sin. Therefore, Paul delivered him to Satan for the destruction of his flesh (probably through sickness), that his spirit might be saved in the day of the Lord. This indicates that once we receive salvation in our spirit, we cannot lose it.

The salvation of our soul, however, is a different matter. Our spirit has been saved in this age, and we cannot lose this salvation. But it is not yet determined whether or not our soul will be saved at the Lord's coming. Unlike the salvation of the spirit, the salvation of the soul is not a matter of simple faith.

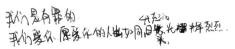

By confessing our sins, believing in the Lord Jesus, and calling on His name, we are regenerated and have salvation in our spirit. But the salvation of the soul requires a long process.

OUR NEED FOR ENJOYMENT

God's intention in His creation of man was that man would take Him in and express Him. Taking in God and expressing God should be man's joy and amusement. Man's happiness and entertainment must be God Himself, and this is not an objective God but a subjective God. To take God in and to live God out is man's joy. We should not blame people for desiring amusement, for God created man with the need for enjoyment. The reason we hunger for food day by day is that we were created with the need to eat. It is impossible to be filled up once with food and never to be hungry again. No, we must eat afresh every day. God created us in this way. In the same principle, God created man with the need for amusement, but our amusement must be God Himself. Because people have lost God, they seek entertainment by going to the movies, theater, and various sporting events. They have not found the fulfillment of their need for entertainment in God Himself. God Himself is the unique fulfillment of our need for entertainment.

THE LOSING AND SAVING OF THE SOUL

All the amusements that people seek outside of God are for the satisfaction of the soul. When they listen to music or enjoy certain sports, they are happy. Many in Hong Kong like to play mah-jongg. To them, that is the best entertainment and enjoyment. Any Christian who still plays mah-jongg is one who is saving his soul. Anyone who has been regenerated in his spirit but still plays mah-jongg will eventually lose his soul at the Lord's coming. For him to refrain from playing mah-jongg is to cause his soul to suffer. Nevertheless, such a Christian needs to lose his soul in the matter of playing mah-jongg. If he does not lose it now, he will lose it when the Lord comes back. The Lord will say to him, "Because you saved your soul so much, now you must lose it." Now we can understand that what the Bible means by losing the soul is for the

soul to lose its enjoyment. Moreover, to save the soul is to pre-
serve the soul in its enjoyment.

If man had expressed God on earth, God would have been
able to recover the earth. Then both man and God would have
enjoyed the earth. God would have been happy, and we would
have been happy also. However, man did not cooperate with
God. Thus, God did not have a way to recover the earth. Rather,
He Himself has even been rejected by the earth. When He came
in the flesh, He was rejected. This present age, the age of the
church, is the age of the world's rejection of Christ. Because
Christ has been rejected, at present He has no joy on this earth.
As His followers, we share His destiny. Our destiny as followers of the Lord Jesus is not to be welcomed by this world;
instead, it is to be rejected. Therefore, this age is not the time
for us to have enjoyment for our soul; it is the time for us to
lose this enjoyment. When the Lord Jesus comes back, that will
be the time for Him to enjoy the earth. Satan will be bound,
Christ will recover the earth, and the entire earth will be under
His reign. At that time Christ will enjoy the earth, and all His
followers will participate in this enjoyment. This is the meaning of Matthew 25:21 and 23, both of which say, "Well done,
good and faithful slave. You were faithful over a few things;
I will set you over many things. Enter into the joy of your
master." This will take place during the millennium when the
Lord Jesus will reclaim the earth and enjoy it. By repossess-
ing the earth, the Lord will have enjoyment. Then He will ask
His followers, His partners, to enter into His joy. This will be
the saving of our soul. In order to have the enjoyment in the
coming age, we need to pay the price in this age by losing our
soul. We need to say, "Lord, for Your sake I don't want to have
so much pleasure or amusement."

THE LOVE OF THE WORLD

After speaking of denying the self, taking up the cross, and
losing the soul, the Lord referred to the world, saying, "What
shall a man be profited if he gains the whole world, but forfeits
his soul-life? Or what shall a man give in exchange for his soul-
life?" (16:26). People love the world simply because it gives
amusement to their soul. They love good clothing, fine cars,

and worldly amusements because they bring enjoyment to the soul. But for the Lord's sake, for the gospel's sake, and for His testimony's sake, we need to be willing to lose the enjoyment of the soul in this age. Are you willing to lose your soulish enjoyment for the Lord's sake? The reason people love the world is that they want to maintain the enjoyment of the soul. Throughout the world there is the enjoyment of the soul. The reason people study to earn a degree is to have a better life, and a better life means more enjoyment. Others work to earn a promotion in their job so that they may have more money for more enjoyment of the soul. When the Lord Jesus came, He lost His soul; that is, He gave up all His soulish enjoyment. He lost the enjoyment of His soul in this age so that He might gain His soul in the coming age. As we have seen, in the coming age the Lord Jesus will enjoy the whole earth. At that time He will invite us, His partners, to share in this enjoyment. We need to wait patiently for the coming enjoyment. If you keep the enjoyment in your soul today, you will lose the enjoyment to come. When some hear this, they may say, "My economy is practical. I care for the present, not for the future." The choice is yours. If you prefer to have your enjoyment today, you are free to do so. But if you save your soul in this age, be assured that you will lose it when the Lord comes back. He will tell you that because you have enjoyed your soul so much, now is the time for you to lose it. Which do you choose—to lose your soul today and gain it tomorrow, or to gain it today and lose it tomorrow? If we could gain the whole world, it would still not be worthwhile to gain it at the cost of losing our soul.

CARING FOR THE LORD'S PLEASURE AND SATISFACTION

We need to be those who care for the Lord's pleasure and satisfaction, and we all must believe the Lord's word. By believing in His word, we were saved. He not only tells us that if we believe in Him, our sins will be forgiven, we shall be cleansed, and we shall have eternal life. His word also tells us that it is not worthwhile to gain the whole world and lose our soul. We should be wise, not foolish. Do not be shortsighted, saying, "I don't care for tomorrow. I care only for today." We must be enlightened by the Lord's word. In the coming age the gaining of the soul will mean a great deal. Even if we had the whole world, we could not buy this. In order to gain the soul in the coming age, it is worthwhile to lose our soulish joy in this age. As long as we have what is necessary for our existence—food, clothing, lodging, and transportation—we should be content. It is sufficient that we can exist and live on earth for the Lord's testimony, loving Him, contacting Him, receiving Him, digesting Him, and living Him out to be His expression. We should be happy with this and not pursue other things. We should be able to say that we do not care for food, clothing, cars, and houses. We live in Him and trust in Him to take care of our needs. But we do not care for today's enjoyment, entertainment, and amusement. Rather, we care for His pleasure and satisfaction. For the Lord's sake, we are willing to drop so many amusements and pleasures. We care to have only what is necessary to exist for His expression. This is what it means to lose the soul for the Lord's sake. If we do this, He will say to us at His coming back, "Well done, good and faithful slave. Enter into the joy of your Master." This is the gaining, the saving, of the soul. If we lose our soul for His sake today, He will reward us with the saving of our soul in the future. But if we save our soul today, we shall lose it in the coming age and suffer some type of punishment. Whether we shall save our soul or lose it in the future depends upon whether we save it or lose it today.

TWO PRACTICAL ILLUSTRATIONS

As the children of God and saints in the Lord, we should love one another. Suppose you have a large savings account in the bank and another brother is very poor and needs help. According to the Lord's sovereignty, this brother's need is brought to your attention. The Lord may burden you to give this brother a large amount of money, but you may be unwilling to do so, not wanting to lose the pleasure of having a certain amount in your bank account. Instead of giving your brother the money the Lord tells you to give, you may reason with the Lord about it, trying to lower the amount. If you do this, you will be saving your soul. Such a thing once happened in China. The Lord burdened one brother to give a certain amount of money to another. But the enemy tempted him to lower the amount. When the brother was enlightened to see the tactics of the enemy, he said, "Satan, if you speak to me about this again, I'll give everything away. I am happy to have nothing in my savings account." To lose our pleasure at having a large savings account is to lose our soul.

You may also either save or lose your soul in buying a suit. To buy a new suit may be an enjoyment to your soul. Will you save your soul by buying an expensive suit, or will you lose it by buying one that is adequate but much less expensive? If you are willing to buy the less expensive suit, you will be able to save some money for the Lord's sake. Even in this small matter you will be losing your soul.

LOSING THE SOUL AND TRANSFORMATION

When we lose our soul and its enjoyment, we are undergoing the process of transformation. Suppose a brother does not care for the Lord in buying a suit. He cares only to satisfy his soulish enjoyment. Such a person cannot be transformed in his disposition, will, or emotion. However, if he cares for the Lord and buys a suit under the leading of the Holy Spirit, his soul will be transformed. The losing of the soul today actually transforms the soul. But the saving of our soul today frustrates the transformation. If we lose our soul in all things related to our daily living, we shall be gradually transformed. Then when the Lord comes back, He will say, "Well done, good slave; come into My joy." At that time your soul will be fully transformed. You will be prepared, perfected, and qualified to enter into the Lord's enjoyment because over the years your soul has been transformed through your willingness to lose the soul. But if you are not willing to lose your soul in this age, your soul will not be transformed.

THE IMPLANTED WORD AND A RICH ENTRANCE

James 1:21 says, "Therefore putting away all filthiness and the abundance of malice, receive in meekness the implanted word, which is able to save your souls." If we are willing to lose our soul, the word will be implanted into our being. The word we have heard in the Bible or in messages will be implanted within us and work for the transformation of our soul. As a result, we shall be rewarded with the saving of our soul when the Lord Jesus comes back. As we lose our soul in all sorts of situations, the word will be implanted into our being to transform our soul. This will make us ready when the Lord Jesus comes back. We shall be transformed and qualified to be the Lord's partners in His reign in the coming kingdom. This is the saving of the soul.

Second Peter 1:11 says, "In this way the entrance into the eternal kingdom of our Lord and Savior Jesus Christ will be richly and bountifully supplied to you." We all need a rich entrance into the eternal kingdom of the Lord. We can have such an entrance by losing our soul today. The more we lose the enjoyment of the soul, the richer an entrance we shall have.

We have seen that although we have been saved in our spirit, we still need the salvation of our soul. Now is the time for us to lose our soul so that we may gain it at the Lord's coming back. We need to lose everything that makes our soul happy. By losing our soul, our entire being will be daily and gradually transformed. Then we shall have the position to be rewarded with the saving of the soul in the future. Outwardly we shall save our soul at the Lord's coming, and inwardly we shall be qualified to participate in the Lord's enjoyment in the coming age.

CHAPTER SEVEN

THE KINGDOM
AS AN EXERCISE AND A REWARD

THE GOAL, THE MATERIAL, AND THE WAY

God's New Testament economy is to build the church with Christ through the kingdom. The church is God's goal, God's desire and destination. His intention is to build the church. As we all know, in order to build anything we need certain material. The material for the building of the church is Christ. Along with the material, we also need the method of building. In Matthew 16 we see the goal, the material, and the method. The goal is the church, the material is Christ, and the method is the kingdom.

After the Lord Jesus had asked His disciples to tell Him who they thought He was, Peter received the revelation that He was the Christ, the Son of the living God. Because it is not adequate simply to have the revelation of Christ, the Lord Jesus went on to say, "I also say to you that you are Peter, and upon this rock I will build My church" (v. 18). When verse 18 is put with verse 16, we have the complete revelation: Christ and the church, the great mystery of God (Eph. 5:32). Christ is for the church. Peter's revelation and the acknowledgment of that revelation are the rock upon which the Lord will build His church. Therefore, the church is the goal, and the Christ revealed and acknowledged by the disciples is the material with which the church is built.

Although in verses 16 and 18 we have the goal and the material, we do not have the way. This is revealed in verse 19, where the Lord said, "I will give to you the keys of the kingdom of the heavens." Exercising the keys of the kingdom is the way to build the church. In other words, the way to build the church is through the kingdom.

CHRIST, THE CHURCH, AND THE KINGDOM

Today the word *church* is used so lightly that it has become virtually meaningless. Many Christians speak of going to church or of belonging to a certain church. But because of the way they use this term, it has no weight or significance. In the New Testament, however, the word *church* is a weighty term. Before Matthew 16 this word is not found in the Bible. In the Gospels the word *church* is used only twice, in Matthew 16 and in Matthew 18. The church is God's goal in the universe. Thus, the church is something very significant, even though Christians have made it appear to be nothing.

If you consider the history of Christianity, you will realize that the enemy has frustrated the believers from Christ and the kingdom. Not many Christians know Christ as He should be known. As we have seen, for the building of the church we need Christ, because Christ is the material for the building. The church can be built only with Christ.

Christians have also been frustrated from knowing the kingdom. Few Christian teachers today speak about the kingdom. If you examine today's Christian publications, you will find very little mention of the kingdom. Fifty years ago, many articles spoke of the kingdom, and those involved in evangelical work even spoke of spreading the kingdom. But today this term is used rarely, because the kingdom has become foreign to our understanding. This is due to the subtlety of the enemy. If we are frustrated from knowing Christ and if we neglect the kingdom, we are through with the church because the church is built with Christ and through the kingdom.

THE EXERCISE OF THE KINGDOM

If you carefully read the New Testament regarding the kingdom, you will see that today the kingdom is an exercise to us. Therefore, we speak of the exercise of the kingdom. The New Testament also reveals clearly that in the future the kingdom will be a reward to us. Thus, the kingdom is an exercise today and a reward in the coming age. The positive reward of the kingdom is to enter into the joy of the Lord. Matthew 25:21 and 23 both say, "Well done, good and faithful slave. You were faithful over a few things; I will set you over many things. Enter into the joy of your master." In the coming age those who receive this positive reward of the kingdom will be co-kings with Christ. We shall no longer be under an exercise; rather, we shall be reigning with Christ. Today, however, is not the time for us to reign, to be the co-kings of Christ. This is for the coming age. For us today, the kingdom is an exercise. Thus, we are not reigning; we are being exercised. This is the reason that we need to lose our soul. To reign is not to lose the soul but to gain the soul. To be poor in spirit and to suffer for the sake of righteousness is not to reign; it is to be exercised.

BEING POOR IN SPIRIT

Matthew 5:3 does not say, "Blessed are the poor in spirit, for theirs will be the kingdom of the heavens." It says, "Blessed are the poor in spirit, for theirs is the kingdom of the heavens." When we are poor in spirit, we are in the exercise of the kingdom. The same is true of those who are persecuted for the sake of righteousness. Verse 10 says, "Blessed are those who are persecuted for the sake of righteousness, for theirs is the kingdom of the heavens." When we are poor in our spirit and when we suffer for the sake of righteousness, we are in the kingdom. To be poor in spirit and to suffer for the sake of righteousness both mean to lose the soul. On the contrary, to be proud and to consider that we are great is to save the soul. To be poor in spirit is to think that we have nothing, know nothing, and are nothing. In a human sense, this is to suffer and to lose the soul. To lose the soul in this way is the real denial of the self. Those who think that they are everything and know everything do not deny the self or lose the soul. The kingdom is not with those who hold this attitude. Whenever we are like this, we are out of the kingdom. We need the mercy and grace of God to say, "Concerning God's economy, I know nothing, I have nothing, and I am nothing. I am nobody." This is what it means to be poor in spirit, to be without human enjoyment, boasting, or pride. As we have pointed out, whenever we are poor in spirit, we are immediately in the kingdom. This is the exercise of the kingdom.

SUFFERING FOR THE SAKE OF RIGHTEOUSNESS

To suffer for the sake of righteousness is definitely to suffer the loss of the enjoyment of the soul. Whenever we are willing to lose the enjoyment of the soul today for the sake of righteousness, we are in the kingdom, and the kingdom is ours. This also is the exercise of the kingdom. It is not a matter of reward or enjoyment, and it is not something we can boast about. Today the entire world is rejecting Christ and the kingdom. The world is also rejecting the followers of Christ. Therefore, we suffer for following Christ, and we lose the enjoyment of our soul today. Because of the kingdom, we are willing to lose our enjoyment. Because of the kingdom, we are willing to deny the self and be poor in spirit. Because of the kingdom, we are willing to be nobody, to know nothing, and to be an empty vessel available to be filled with Christ for the building of the church.

Matthew 5:10 speaks of suffering for the sake of righteousness because, according to the Bible, the kingdom as a whole is a matter of righteousness. Thus, to suffer for the sake of righteousness is to suffer for the sake of the kingdom. If we suffer for the sake of the kingdom, if we are willing to lose our soulish enjoyment today, we are in the kingdom. There is no need for us to enter into the kingdom, for we are in the kingdom already. But what aspect of the kingdom are we in? We are not in the reigning aspect but in the aspect of exercise. To repeat, the reigning aspect of the kingdom is coming, but the aspect of the exercise of the kingdom is present today.

THE CHURCH BUILT UP THROUGH THE KINGDOM

Now we need to see how the kingdom is the way the church is built. According to our experience in the church life, we all have realized that the church cannot be built up with those who refuse to deny themselves. Today not only the worldly people but even Christians are fighting with one another. In every society and organization people think of themselves as being somebody and as having something. This is even true of children in kindergarten. Where can you find a place where people always have the attitude that they are nothing and have nothing and that they are empty vessels? Such people can be found only in the church. If we cannot find people with such an attitude in the church, then there is a question whether that really is the church. The church can only be built up through the kingdom, which we have seen is today an exercise. The Gospel of Matthew reveals that this exercise kills every part of our being. When some hear this, they may say, "The denial of the self is difficult enough. Now you are telling us that the exercise of the kingdom will kill every part of our being. We cannot bear this." Humanly speaking, I can only agree with you and sympathize with you because I am the same.

THE EYE OF THE NEEDLE

In Matthew 19 the Lord Jesus illustrated how difficult it is for us to enter into the kingdom (v. 24). He said that it was even more difficult than for a camel to go through the eye of a needle. Humanly speaking, no one can enter into the kingdom. As far as we are concerned, it is impossible. But what is impossible with men is possible with God. God has the way for us to enter into the kingdom. His way is not to enlarge the eye of the needle and make it a wide gate so that even a heavily laden camel can get through. Rather, His way is to reduce the size of the camel until it is thin enough to pass through the eye of the needle. It is possible for thin thread to pass through the eye of the needle.

In order for us to pass through the eye of the needle, the Lord must make us as thin as thread. By nature, we are camels. But God has a way to spin us into thin thread. Although I have been a Christian for more than fifty years, I am still in the eye of the needle. Sometimes I have cried out, "Lord, I cannot tolerate Your spinning any longer." But the Lord said, "Be patient, for I am helping you. You are still too thick. I am spinning you to make you thinner." There were times when I wanted to be cut off from this spinning process. But at those times the Lord said to me, "It is not up to you. You may want to be cut off, but what will you use to do the cutting? The scissors are not in your hands. I shall neither drop you nor cut you off.

Rather, I shall keep on spinning you." This is the exercise of the kingdom today.

THE EXPERIENCE OF CHRIST

Many years ago we received help regarding this matter of the kingdom. Because we were helped by this, we ministered it to others. There were various reactions to what we ministered concerning the exercise and reward of the kingdom. Some said that it was Hinduism, and others that it was similar to the Catholic teaching of purgatory. But this is not Hinduism, purgatory, or any form of asceticism. It is the experience of Christ.

THE MIND OF CHRIST

Philippians 2:5 says, "Let this mind be in you, which was also in Christ Jesus." The mind of Christ needs to become our mind. After Paul tells us that we need to let the mind of Christ become ours, he speaks of how the Lord Jesus was willing to become small and lowly. This is what we mean by spinning. The heavenly, divine spinning brought Christ down from the heavens to the earth. It caused the great Christ to become less than the lowest and smallest. Christ has been spun. He was willing to be spun in this way, for His mind was that kind of mind.

We need to consider the context behind Paul's word to the Philippians regarding the mind of Christ. To a certain degree at least, the believers at Philippi were not in the kingdom. In their thinking they were regarding themselves as better and higher than others. That was an indication that they did not have the mind of Christ. Thus, the apostle Paul told them that they needed to allow the mind of Christ to become their mind. He pointed out that although Christ was so high and great, He was willing to become lowly and even to be put to death on the cross. When Christ was crucified, He was made nothing. The enemy even challenged Him to come down from the cross. Those who mocked Him said that if He would come down from the cross, they would believe in Him. What a devilish challenge that was! Instead of coming down from the cross, Christ remained there for at least six hours to be nothing. He did not say one word to vindicate Himself. This is the mind of

Christ, the only mind good for the building of the church. Only when we have such a mind are we qualified for the building.

WILLING TO BECOME NOTHING

If we see this vision and compare it with the situation among the Christians today, we shall realize that the building up of the church is a human impossibility. Perhaps you will say, "Lord, when You were on earth, You said that You would build Your church. But nearly two thousand years have passed, and still we do not see the building. Lord, where is Your building?" If we speak to the Lord like this, He may reply, "You do not see the building because so few have been willing to care for the exercise of the kingdom." We all love the Lord and the church. But the question is whether or not we are willing to become nothing. As we all know, our spirit is the very depth of our being. To be poor in this part of our being means to realize that we are nothing. Are you willing to be nothing?

THE NEED FOR THE EXERCISE OF THE KINGDOM

Take the example of washing dishes. Sometimes I wash the dishes for my wife. But many times I have had the thought that I would like the young people to know what I am doing and to realize what a good example I am setting for them. This is the magnified self. I know that this is the attitude among many in the brothers' houses. As you are washing dishes, you may say, "Lord, You know that the others are not willing to do the dishes. But I am doing them, Lord, for Your sake." This is the ugly self expressed in the washing of dishes. When you wash the dishes and have no thought or feeling about it, that is an indication that the self is gone. It reveals that you are nothing in the matter of washing the dishes. But as long as we have some thought concerning ourselves in this matter, it is a clear sign that self is present. Not only is self present; it is nourished. After some have washed the dishes in such a way, they go into their room and pray, "Lord, thank You that I was the only one to wash the dishes." This kind of giving thanks comes from the magnified self. If you wash the dishes in this way for several days, you will eventually become angry with those you are living with and no longer wash any dishes. This is an indication of how much we need the exercise of the kingdom.

THE GRACE OF GOD

What is sown in the Gospels grows in the Epistles and is harvested in Revelation. In the Epistles we have the excellent example of the apostle Paul. In 1 Corinthians 15:10 Paul says, "By the grace of God I am what I am; and His grace unto me did not turn out to be in vain, but, on the contrary, I labored more abundantly than all of them, yet not I but the grace of God which is with me." It was by the grace of God that Paul was what he was, and by this grace he labored more than others. Grace is God as our enjoyment. When we put 1 Corinthians 15:10 together with certain verses from the book of Philippians, we see that grace is nothing less than the incarnated, crucified, and resurrected Christ becoming the life-giving Spirit. Thus, in Philippians 1:19 Paul says, "I know that for me this will turn out to salvation through your petition and the bountiful supply of the Spirit of Jesus Christ." This is the grace of God. The grace of God is the bountiful, exhaustless, unending supply of the Spirit of Jesus Christ. Today this Spirit is within us. Therefore, Paul could say, "I am able to do all things in Him who empowers me" (4:13). Here Paul seemed to be saying, "I cannot do anything, but I can do all things through Him who empowers me. The One who empowers me is not in the heavens; He is within me. In Him, I can do all things."

WORKING OUT OUR SALVATION

In Philippians 2:12 Paul says, "Work out your own salvation with fear and trembling." This is not eternal salvation but the salvation of the soul, the salvation of the kingdom. It is the salvation to receive the reward and to enter into the joy of the Lord in the coming age. This salvation needs to be worked out by us, whereas the eternal salvation does not require our work. Regarding eternal salvation, we simply receive it and have it. But we need to work something out in order to have the salvation of the soul, the salvation that qualifies us to receive the reward of the kingdom. In ourselves we are not able to work out this salvation. But we have One in us who can work it out. This One is God Himself who is working within us both the willing and the working for His good pleasure (v. 13). God works in, and we work out. His inward working requires our willing cooperation. If we are willing to cooperate with Him, He will have the ground and the way to work within us so that we may work out our salvation. There is no need for us to strive or use our own effort to accomplish such a salvation.

PREACHING THE GOSPEL OF THE KINGDOM

As we all know, we must eat in order to have strength. The problem is not with the food, for the food has been prepared and is now in front of us. People may do many things for you, but no one can eat for you. In God's New Testament economy He first saved us and then put us into the exercise of the kingdom. For this exercise we need Christ and the bountiful supply of the Spirit of Jesus Christ. Although this Spirit is present within all real believers, millions of Christians are not hungry. Therefore, we who are hungry and who are eating Christ must preach the gospel of the kingdom. We need to tell the saints that although they have been saved for eternity, they may nevertheless have a problem with the Lord at the time of His coming back to settle accounts. The Lord will examine our living, behavior, and work since our salvation. This is a serious matter.

The gospel of the kingdom has been completely buried by the enemy. Today we must sound the trumpet of this gospel. When the Lord comes back, He will establish His kingdom of righteousness. At that time He will give us either a positive reward or a negative reward according to our doings. These doings are related to three matters: the denying of the self, the taking up of the cross, and the losing of the soul. The way we deal with these three things will be the basis on which the Lord will settle accounts with us. Then He will decide whether we shall receive a positive reward or a negative one. As those who believe the Bible, we must recognize that such a judgment is coming.

The gospel of the kingdom is for the building of the church. Many Christians today, including some of us in the Lord's recovery, may be ignorant or negligent of this. It is not sufficient to talk about spirituality. The question is whether or not we are taking Christ as our supply to deny the self, bear the cross, and lose our soul. The reward of the kingdom in the future is an incentive for the building of the church. It is also a warning regarding the building of the church. If we do not live a life that is crucified, resurrected, and overcoming, a life that denies the self, takes up the cross, and loses the soul, we must be warned of the danger of being disapproved.

RUNNING THE RACE
AND PRESSING TOWARD THE PRIZE

In 1 Corinthians 9:24-27 Paul says that he was running the race. In this portion of the Word he tells us clearly that he was concerned for himself. First Corinthians 9:27 says, "I buffet my body and make it my slave, lest perhaps having preached to others, I myself may become disapproved." Paul realized that although he was preaching the gospel of the kingdom to others, he himself might be disapproved, that is, be cast away. Some versions use the word *disqualified.* In a race some are qualified and others are disqualified; some are approved and others are disapproved. If we are approved, we shall gain the prize, which is the crown. But if we are disapproved, we shall be cast away and not receive the crown.

In Philippians 3 Paul says clearly that he did not count himself to have laid hold. In verses 13 and 14 he says, "Brothers, I do not account of myself to have laid hold; but one thing I do: Forgetting the things which are behind and stretching forward to the things which are before, I pursue toward the goal for the prize to which God in Christ Jesus has called me upward." The way Paul was pressing toward the prize was by knowing Christ, the power of His resurrection, and the fellowship of His sufferings. He wanted to know how Christ suffered for the kingdom, and he wanted to share in that suffering. Paul realized that Christ had been spun into thin thread, and he wanted to be the same as He, even conformed to His death. Christ had been crucified on the cross to become nothing, and Paul also wanted to become nothing. Paul realized that in himself he could not attain to this. He had to know the power of Christ's resurrection. Therefore, Paul says that he could do all things in Him who empowered him. This One, the resurrected One, today is the life-giving Spirit. He is the bountiful supply within us. If we are willing to cooperate with Him and open to Him, He will fill us to the brim. The tide of the bountiful supply of the Spirit will fill us and flood us. There will not even be the need for us to swim, for the tide will flood us and carry us on.

In 2 Timothy 4:6 Paul says that he was already being poured out as a drink offering. The next two verses say, "I have fought the good fight; I have finished the course; I have kept the faith. Henceforth there is laid up for me the crown of righteousness, with which the Lord, the righteous Judge, will recompense me in that day." Notice in verse 8 that Paul does not speak of a crown of mercy, grace, or love, but a crown of righteousness. In 2 Timothy 4:18 he says, "The Lord will deliver me from every evil work and will save me into His heavenly kingdom." Here the apostle Paul even uses the term *heavenly kingdom*. This refers to the reward of the kingdom. No doubt, Paul will be one of the co-kings with Christ, one reigning over the nations during the thousand years. That will be Paul's reward and enjoyment.

THE PARTICULAR ENJOYMENT OF CHRIST

To receive the kingdom reward is to have the uttermost enjoyment of the Lord in a particular way. Today we enjoy Christ, and in eternity we also shall enjoy Christ. But the Christ we enjoy today and shall enjoy in eternity is the common portion. After the millennium Christ will be the common portion to all His believers. But during the millennium He will be a particular portion to the overcomers, to His co-kings. This particular portion will be the prize, the reward, to His faithful followers. This is the reward of the kingdom, which is altogether a matter of enjoyment. Today we have a marvelous foretaste of the sweetness of enjoying Christ. But if we exercise ourselves in the kingdom today, the topmost, particular portion of the enjoyment of Christ will be ours.

THE JOY OF THE EXERCISE OF THE KINGDOM

Even today, as we are under the exercise of the kingdom,

we are enjoying Christ. Apparently, it is not a pleasant matter to deny the self, to take up the cross, and to lose the soul. However, when we enter into the exercise of the kingdom, all this becomes an enjoyment. Once you have tasted it, you will never want to leave it. You will desire to deny yourself because the best enjoyment of Christ is in self-denial and in the losing of the soul. If you do not believe me, I ask you to try it. Some may say, "This sounds like Hinduism. I don't want to suffer this." If you hold this attitude, you will find it difficult to pray or to smile inwardly. The only smile you will have will be an outward, manufactured smile. You may claim to be happy, but you will have no happiness deep within. But those who are willing to take Christ as their life by His bountiful supply, denying the self, taking up the cross, and losing the soul, will be full of joy. What joy they will have! When the time comes for them to praise the Lord, their joy will burst forth. Which do you prefer—an outward smile or this deep joy?

I am not an angel; rather, I am a human being. At times I may be offended by a brother. However, if I do not deny myself, bear the cross, and lose the soul when I am offended, I shall be saving my soul. Whenever I save my soul like this, I cannot pray or read the Bible well. Furthermore, I cannot even sit comfortably or rest well. But if, by the Lord's mercy and grace, I take Christ as my bountiful supply and live by Him, exercising myself under the kingdom, I shall lose my soul. I deny myself, take up my cross, and have joy. This is the enjoyment of Christ.

To deny the self, to take up the cross, and to lose the soul is not a Hindu teaching or a form of asceticism. On the contrary, it is an enjoyment of Christ Himself deep in our inward being. What comfort and intimacy this is! How real is the presence of Christ! This is the enjoyment of the exercise of the kingdom. This will qualify us to receive the reward of the kingdom so that we may enter into the highest enjoyment of Christ in His millennial reign.

The matter of the exercise of the kingdom should not merely be a teaching to us. It must be our genuine experience today for the building of the church. If we continue in this exercise, the kingdom will be ours, the church will spontaneously be built up, we shall be qualified to reign with Christ in the kingdom, and we shall be rewarded with the special enjoyment of Christ in the coming age.

As an exercise, the kingdom is ours today, and we are in it (Matt. 5:3, 10). As a reward, the kingdom will be our enjoyment in the future, and we shall enter into it (v. 20; 18:3). In the exercise of the kingdom today, we are under the heavenly ruling; but in the reward of the kingdom in the next age, we shall rule as kings over the nations. Hence, in the exercise of the kingdom today, being ruled by the heavens, we are losing our soul, that is, losing the enjoyment of our soul; but in the reward of the kingdom in the future, ruling over the nations, we shall save our soul, that is, gain the enjoyment of our soul.

CHAPTER EIGHT

THE INCENTIVE TO SEEK CHRIST

God's intention is to build the church with Christ. Christ is the unique material for the building of the church. However, in His sovereignty, God knew that His chosen people would not have an adequate desire to seek Christ. This is the actual situation among Christians today. Although many have received Christ as their Savior and are saved, they do not seek Christ. But because God's desire is to build the church with Christ, Christ must be wrought into our being. We need to be saturated and permeated with Christ in order to become a part of Christ. When we have been saturated, soaked, and permeated with Christ, we shall each be a part of Christ. When all these parts are put together, they constitute the church.

GAINING CHRIST

Although there are millions of genuinely saved Christians, so many have gone no farther than receiving Christ as their Savior. They do not care about the subjective Christ but leave Christ in the heavens as an objective Savior in whom they believe and whom they worship. They do not seek Christ, and they do not go on to attain unto Christ or to gain Christ.

This matter of gaining Christ is fully revealed in Philippians chapter 3. In Philippians 3:8 the apostle Paul says, "Moreover I also count all things to be loss on account of the excellency of the knowledge of Christ Jesus my Lord, on account of whom I have suffered the loss of all things and count them as refuse that I may gain Christ." Even Paul felt that he was void of Christ, short of Christ. Although he had experienced Christ to such a degree, he still said that he was stretching forward to gain more of Christ.

HUNGRY FOR CHRIST

I would ask you to consider how many Christians today are this intent in their seeking after Christ. How many Christians are hungry and thirsty for Christ? I doubt that among us there are very many who pursue Christ in this way. To tell you the truth, in recent days I have been asking myself how hungry I am for Christ. I have said to myself, "Are you hungry for Christ? You have been in the ministry for more than forty-five years, and you have been in the church life for such a long time. Are you as hungry for Christ as the apostle Paul was in Philippians 3?" I must confess and say to the Lord, "Lord, have mercy on me. I am not that hungry or that seeking." Philippians 3 reveals how hungry Paul was for Christ. In verses 10 and 11 he says, "To know Him and the power of His resurrection and the fellowship of His sufferings, being conformed to His death, if perhaps I may attain to the out-resurrection from the dead." Here we see that Paul had a great hunger for Christ. How many Christians today are this hungry to gain Christ?

It is important that we realize who Christ is today. Christ is the Triune God processed through incarnation, human living, crucifixion, resurrection, and ascension to be the life-giving Spirit. Such a Spirit is here with us right now. Everything positive is included in this life-giving Spirit. Within Him there is redemption, forgiveness, justification, righteousness, holiness, life, light, and power. In the life-giving Spirit there is God, man, and every positive thing in the universe.

GOD'S DESIRE

God's desire is that we first receive Christ. When we do, we are redeemed, justified, reconciled, forgiven, washed, regenerated, and saved. After we have been saved, God wants us to hunger after Christ. We need to be able to say, "Oh, I want to gain more Christ! I must be a person hungry for Christ, that Christ may be my life supply and that I may be filled, saturated, permeated, and soaked with Him. Then I shall become a part of Christ." It is in this way that the church is built with Christ.

PREACHING THE GOSPEL OF THE KINGDOM

The reason very few Christians are hungry for Christ is that the gospel of the kingdom has never been preached adequately. What we all have heard is only the gospel of grace, not the gospel of the kingdom. We all have heard the gospel of grace regarding eternal salvation. We have believed this gospel, and we have received eternal salvation. But perhaps we have never heard an adequate preaching of the gospel of the kingdom. Thus, we all, including me, need a serious warning.

In George Whitefield's biography we are told that one day when he was preaching on the subject of hell, someone in the congregation leaped into the aisle and began to shout that he was falling into hell. This indicates how prevailing was Whitefield's preaching about hell. Today we need some preachers to proclaim the punishment of the kingdom in just such a prevailing way. We need to warn the believers about being cast into outer darkness where there will be weeping and gnashing of teeth. We need to preach the warning gospel of the kingdom to stir up the Christians regarding God's dispensational punishment. This type of preaching compels us to seek Christ.

A good evangelist always preaches the gospel from two angles. The first angle is to warn people that if they do not repent and believe in the Lord Jesus, they will be cast into hell to suffer the punishment of eternal fire. People need to be told of the judgment of the righteous God. The other angle is to tell people how Christ has done everything to save them and that they simply need to receive Him. The principle is the same in the preaching of the gospel of the kingdom. We need to warn all the Christians that one day Christ will come back to settle accounts with them. At that time they will be either rewarded or punished, either brought into the bright enjoyment with Christ or cast into outer darkness. Thousands of unbelievers and sinners have been compelled to believe out of the fear of going to hell. In like manner, Christians need to be compelled to seek Christ out of the fear of the coming judgment.

The promise of the kingdom reward is also a great incentive to seek Christ. The hope of receiving this reward encourages us to gain Him. When we are compelled to seek after Christ and encouraged to gain Christ, we shall be hungry for Christ. We shall earnestly desire to gain Christ so that we may attain to the out-resurrection from the dead.

STIRRED UP TO SEEK CHRIST IN A DESPERATE WAY

When we have been compelled and encouraged to seek Christ, we shall not be idle regarding Christ, and we shall no longer be indifferent. I must confess that I have a burden about this matter. I am concerned that not even many of us have been stirred up to seek Christ in such a desperate way. We need to see how crucial the situation is. We shall either be punished or rewarded. Thus, we need to say, "Lord, I am desperate. Because I will be either punished or rewarded, I must seek after You." This is not simply a matter of knowing the truth of the kingdom. It is a matter of being desperate to gain Christ.

Are you seeking Christ? Are you gaining Him more and more? If not, do not make excuses for yourself. Do not say, "Lord, I can't make it. I can't come up to the standard of Your constitution in Matthew 5, 6, and 7. Lord, You know that no one can do it. How can I make it? Lord, please excuse me." You may excuse yourself today, but you will not be able to do so when you meet the Lord at His judgment seat. At that time there will be no excuse. If you try to excuse yourself then, the Lord will say, "Did I not present Myself to you? I am the all-sufficient grace. But were you hungry enough to seek Me?" What will you say? You will be silent.

Because so few Christians are hungry for the subjective Christ, it is impossible for the church to be built up with them. Where can you find Christians who are denying the self and losing the soul? It is difficult to find any. Most Christians stay with a particular group as long as they are happy there. But when they are no longer happy, they leave and go somewhere else. This indicates that there is no denying of the self and no losing of the soul. Instead, there is one excuse after another. But what about us? Are we making excuses, or are we being forced to seek Christ? We need to tell the Lord that we are short of Him and that we are desperate to gain Him.

PAUL, THE PATTERN

I thank the Lord for setting up a pattern in the New Testament with the apostle Paul (1 Tim. 1:16). Paul was so hungry for Christ that eventually he became fully saturated with Christ. Therefore, in Philippians Paul seemed to be saying, "As long as I can manifest Christ, I don't care about the circumstances, for to me, to live is Christ. I am satisfied to be able to manifest Christ in any environment." Paul was one who sought Christ in an absolute way. He was utterly hungry for Christ, and he did everything possible to gain Christ, to experience Christ, and to be saturated with Christ. Therefore, from his experience he could say that it was God who operated in him both the willing and the working for His good pleasure (2:13). He could also say, "I am able to do all things in Him who empowers me" (4:13). At the end of his life, Paul had the assurance to say these words: "The Lord will deliver me from every evil work and will save me into His heavenly kingdom" (2 Tim. 4:18). No doubt, Paul was saturated with Christ. He surely was one fully built into the Body of Christ and completely under the exercise of the kingdom.

A DESCRIPTION OF THE LIFE OF CHRIST

Recently, a brother testified in a meeting that the constitution of the kingdom of the heavens in Matthew 5, 6, and 7 is a description of the life of Christ. I appreciate this word. All the exercises and requirements of the kingdom are a description of Christ's life. They all speak of how much Christ's life can do in us. The requirements of the kingdom's constitution and the exercise of the kingdom reveal what great things Christ's life can accomplish in us. Thus, there is no excuse. His grace is all-sufficient. If Christ had not been incarnated, crucified, and resurrected, we might have an excuse. But now, after having been incarnated, crucified, resurrected, and ascended, Christ is the very all-inclusive life-giving Spirit within us. The only question is whether or not we are hungry for Him and seek after Him. Do not make excuses for not denying the self, taking up the cross, or losing the soul. None of us should offer excuses for ourselves. Instead, we should say, "Lord, there is no excuse. I am compelled to seek You, and I am encouraged to gain You. Lord, I want to be filled with You, saturated with You, and permeated with You so that I may be a part of You."

THE EXERCISE AND THE REWARD

If we are filled, saturated, and permeated with Christ, we shall spontaneously be under the exercise of the kingdom. As we read Paul's Epistles, we see that he was constantly denying himself. His life was also a life of bearing the cross and losing the soul. This was not done by asceticism but by the all-inclusive life-giving Spirit living within Paul. Paul enjoyed Christ as the life-giving Spirit to the uttermost; he hungered after Him and constantly enjoyed Him. Paul's enjoyment of Christ spontaneously brought him into the exercise of the kingdom. This enabled him to fulfill all the requirements of the constitution of the kingdom of the heavens.

Paul was in the exercise of the kingdom for the church. There is only one class of people with whom the church can be built: those who are in the exercise of the kingdom. If we mean business with the Lord for the building of the church, we must be hungry to be saturated with Christ as the all-inclusive life-giving Spirit. By being saturated with the life-giving Spirit, we are brought under the exercise of the kingdom. Then we have the kingdom life.

The exercise of the kingdom is the actuality of the church life today. To a great degree, what we have is still the appearance. We are yet void of the reality. The reality of the church life is the exercise of the kingdom, and the genuine exercise of the kingdom comes through the adequate enjoyment of Christ. Through this enjoyment and exercise, we are built up together as the church. This is Christ building His church with Himself through the kingdom.

Matthew 5:3 says, "Blessed are the poor in spirit, for theirs is the kingdom of the heavens"; and Matthew 5:10 says, "Blessed are those who are persecuted for the sake of righteousness, for theirs is the kingdom of the heavens." If we are poor in spirit and are persecuted for the sake of righteousness, the kingdom is ours, and we are in it today. But what aspect of the kingdom are we in, in the aspect of reward or the aspect of exercise? We are in the aspect of the exercise of the kingdom. Matthew 5:20 says, "I say to you that unless your righteousness surpasses that of the scribes and Pharisees, you shall by no means enter into the kingdom of the heavens," and Matthew 7:21 says, "Not everyone who says to Me, Lord, Lord, will enter into the kingdom of the heavens, but he who does the will of My Father who is in the heavens." Both of these verses speak of entering into the kingdom of the heavens in the future. On the one hand, the kingdom is ours, and we are in it already; on the other hand, the kingdom is coming, and we shall enter into it. With respect to the exercise of the kingdom, we are in it today. But with respect to the reward of the kingdom, we shall enter into it in the future.

THE WILL OF GOD

After saying that only those who do the will of the Father will enter into the kingdom of the heavens, the Lord said, "Many will say to Me in that day, Lord, Lord, was it not in Your name that we prophesied, and in Your name cast out demons, and in Your name did many works of power? And then I will declare to them: I never knew you. Depart from Me, you workers of lawlessness" (vv. 22-23). Here the Lord seemed to be saying, "Get away from Me, you lawless ones. Whatever you did was lawlessness. You were not doing the will of God, and you were not hungry for Me." Here we see that it is not a matter of doing things or of working but of enjoying Christ. This is the will of God. The will of God is that we enjoy Christ and be built up so that the church may exist on earth.

A WARNING AND AN INCENTIVE

We have seen that, on the one hand, we are in the exercise of the kingdom and that, on the other hand, we shall enter into the reward of the kingdom. This fact must be both a warning and an incentive to us. It must compel us, attract us, and encourage us to seek Christ. However, we still may not have a sufficient appetite. We may not yet be hungry for Christ, and we may not take this warning and incentive seriously. Instead, we may be indifferent or negligent. But we need to say, "Lord, have mercy on me. I am hungry for You, and I want to gain You more and more. I want to gain You so that I may arrive at the out-resurrection from among the dead." This resurrection from the dead, mentioned by Paul in Philippians 3, is the reward of the kingdom. I hope that we shall be stirred up to realize that this is not an insignificant matter.

In this chapter you have heard a warning and an incentive. Whether you will accept it or not, whether you will be hungry for Christ and seek Christ or not, is your responsibility.

ABOUT THE AUTHOR

Witness Lee was born in 1905 in northern China and raised in a Christian family. At age nineteen he was fully captured for Christ and immediately consecrated himself to preach the gospel for the rest of his life. Early in his service, he met Watchman Nee, a renowned preacher, teacher, and writer. Witness Lee labored together with Watchman Nee under his direction. In 1934 Watchman Nee entrusted Witness Lee with the responsibility for his publication operation, called the Shanghai Gospel Book Room.

Prior to the Communist takeover in 1949, Witness Lee was sent by Watchman Nee and his other co-workers to Taiwan to ensure that the things delivered to them by the Lord would not be lost. Watchman Nee instructed Witness Lee to continue the former's publishing operation abroad as the Taiwan Gospel Book Room, which has been publicly recognized as the publisher of Watchman Nee's works outside China. Witness Lee's work in Taiwan manifested the Lord's abundant blessing. From a mere three hundred fifty believers, newly fled from the mainland, the churches in Taiwan grew to twenty thousand believers in five years.

In 1962 Witness Lee felt led of the Lord to move to the United States, and he began to minister in Los Angeles in December of that year. During his thirty-five years of service throughout the United States, he ministered in weekly meetings, weekend conferences, and weeklong trainings, delivering several thousand spoken messages. His speaking has since been published, and many of his books have been translated into numerous languages. He gave his last public conference in February 1997 at the age of ninety-one and went to be with the Lord, whom he loved and served, on June 9, 1997. Witness Lee leaves behind a prolific presentation of the truth in the Bible. His major work, *Life-study of the Bible,* the fruit of his labor from 1974 to 1995, comprises over twenty-five thousand pages of commentary on every book of the Bible from the perspective of the believers' enjoyment and experience of God's divine life in Christ through the Holy Spirit. In addition, *The Collected Works of Witness Lee* contains over one hundred thirty volumes (over seventy-five thousand pages) of his other ministry from 1932 to 1997. Witness Lee was also the chief editor of a new translation of the New Testament into Chinese called the Recovery Version, and he directed the translation of the English New Testament Recovery Version. The Recovery Version also appears in over twenty-five other languages. In the Recovery Version he provided an extensive body of footnotes, outlines, and spiritual cross references. A radio broadcast of his messages can be heard on Christian radio stations in the United States and Europe. In 1965 Witness Lee founded Living Stream Ministry, a non-profit corporation, located in Anaheim, California, which publishes his and Watchman Nee's ministry.

Witness Lee's ministry emphasizes the experience of Christ as life and the practical oneness of the believers as the Body of Christ. Stressing the importance of attending to both of these matters, he led the churches under his care to grow in Christian life and function. He was unbending in his conviction that God's goal is not narrow sectarianism but the universal Body of Christ. In time, believers everywhere began to meet simply as the church in their localities in response to this conviction. Through his ministry hundreds of local churches have been raised up throughout the earth.

OTHER BOOKS PUBLISHED BY
Living Stream Ministry

Titles by Witness Lee:

Abraham—Called by God	978-0-7363-0359-0
The Experience of Life	978-0-87083-417-2
The Knowledge of Life	978-0-87083-419-6
The Tree of Life	978-0-87083-300-7
The Economy of God	978-0-87083-415-8
The Divine Economy	978-0-87083-268-0
God's New Testament Economy	978-0-87083-199-7
The World Situation and God's Move	978-0-87083-092-1
Christ vs. Religion	978-0-87083-010-5
The All-inclusive Christ	978-0-87083-020-4
Gospel Outlines	978-0-87083-039-6
Character	978-0-87083-322-9
The Secret of Experiencing Christ	978-0-87083-227-7
The Life and Way for the Practice of the Church Life	978-0-87083-785-2
The Basic Revelation in the Holy Scriptures	978-0-87083-105-8
The Crucial Revelation of Life in the Scriptures	978-0-87083-372-4
The Spirit with Our Spirit	978-0-87083-798-2
Christ as the Reality	978-0-87083-047-1
The Central Line of the Divine Revelation	978-0-87083-960-3
The Full Knowledge of the Word of God	978-0-87083-289-5
Watchman Nee—A Seer of the Divine Revelation ...	978-0-87083-625-1

Titles by Watchman Nee:

How to Study the Bible	978-0-7363-0407-8
God's Overcomers	978-0-7363-0433-7
The New Covenant	978-0-7363-0088-9
The Spiritual Man • 3 volumes	978-0-7363-0269-2
Authority and Submission	978-0-7363-0185-5
The Overcoming Life	978-1-57593-817-2
The Glorious Church	978-0-87083-745-6
The Prayer Ministry of the Church	978-0-87083-860-6
The Breaking of the Outer Man and the Release ...	978-1-57593-955-1
The Mystery of Christ	978-1-57593-954-4
The God of Abraham, Isaac, and Jacob	978-0-87083-932-0
The Song of Songs	978-0-87083-872-9
The Gospel of God • 2 volumes	978-1-57593-953-7
The Normal Christian Church Life	978-0-87083-027-3
The Character of the Lord's Worker	978-1-57593-322-1
The Normal Christian Faith	978-0-87083-748-7
Watchman Nee's Testimony	978-0-87083-051-8

Available at
Christian bookstores, or contact Living Stream Ministry
2431 W. La Palma Ave. • Anaheim, CA 92801
1-800-549-5164 • www.livingstream.com